Pastor Josh,
  Thank you for your leadership & care for people with disabilities. We are grateful for your long term partnership!
"Hope Lives!"

Tim + Marie

Nathaniel's Hope

TM

Hope
Lives

LITTLE LIFE. BIG PURPOSE.
Seeing a new view from a
child with special needs

TIM & MARIE KUCK

HigherLife Development Services, Inc.
PO Box 623307
Oviedo, Florida 32762
(407) 563-4806
www.ahigherlife.com

Printed in the United States of America
10 9 8 7 6 5 4 3 2 1

Library of Congress Cataloging-in-Publication Data

Paperback: ISBN 978-1-7337273-3-4
Hardback: ISBN 978-1-7337273-4-1
eBook: ISBN 978-1-7337273-5-8

Scripture quotations marked CEV are from the Contemporary English Version, copyright © 1995 by the American Bible Society. Used by permission.

Scripture quotations marked ESV are taken from the ESV® Bible (The Holy Bible, English Standard Version®). ESV® Text Edition: 2016. Copyright © 2001 by Crossway, a publishing ministry of Good News Publishers. The ESV® text has been reproduced in cooperation with and by permission of Good News Publishers.

Scriptures marked GNT are taken from the Good News Translation - Second Edition © 1992 by American Bible Society. Used by permission.

Scripture quotations marked NAS are from the New American Standard Bible, copyright © 1960, 1962, 1963, 1968, 1971, 1972, 1973, 1975, 1977, 1995 by The Lockman Foundation. Used by permission. (www.Lockman.org)

Scripture quotations marked NIV are taken from the Holy Bible, NEW INTERNATIONAL VERSION®, NIV® Copyright © 1973, 1978, 1984, 2011 by Biblica, Inc.® Used by permission. All rights reserved worldwide.

Scripture quotations marked NLT are from the Holy Bible, New Living Translation, copyright © 1996, 2004, 2007. Used by permission of Tyndale House Publishers, Inc., Wheaton, IL 60189. All rights reserved.

Scripture quotations marked NKJV are from the New King James Version of the Bible. Copyright © 1979, 1980, 1982 by Thomas Nelson, Inc., publishers. Used by permission.

Scripture quotations marked TLB are from The Living Bible. Copyright © 1971. Used by permission of Tyndale House Publishers, Inc., Wheaton, IL 60189. All rights reserved.

ENDORSEMENTS

"*Hope Lives* tells the story of God's faithfulness and grace in the midst of pain and suffering, all through the eyes of Nathaniel, a child with special needs. Whether you are going through hard times or not, this book will give you hope."

– Tony Dungy
Super Bowl-Winning Coach and NBC Sports Analyst

"Any child can easily influence others on the playground, but only a few influence a world—one of those is Nathaniel. His remarkable little life, although short and difficult, has touched countless special-needs families around the world, bringing hope and building bridges between the broken and the whole, the weak and the strong. If you are searching for hope, Nathaniel's story has more than enough for you...read it and be blessed!"

– Joni Eareckson Tada
Joni and Friends International Disability Center

"*Hope Lives* is more than an endearing personal account of a special-needs child's impact on his family and the world; it is a devotional that helps our faith grow deeper and higher. We were made to love, for God is love, and we were each made in His image. This wonderful book helps us love in profound and practical ways."

– Dr. Joel C. Hunter
Faith Community Organizer; Former Senior Pastor of
Northland, A Church Distributed

"Uniquely told from the perspective of Nathaniel, a boy born with special needs, *Hope Lives* will capture your heart and mind. You will understand just how valuable, purposeful, and love-filled a life lived with disabilities can be in the lives of others. Once you begin reading this book, you won't be able to put it down. You will see genuine, God-given hope in real lives. You will be inspired to come alongside families affected by special needs with Christ-like understanding, compassion, and hope."

– Shawn Thornton
Author and Senior Pastor, Calvary Community Church,
Westlake Village, California

"I just couldn't put this charming book down. I sat there reading, laughing, and crying. Thank you Tim and Marie, for sharing Nathaniel with us all. His life continues to bring joy to so many."

– Emily Colson
Speaker, Author, Mom to Max

"Because of Nathaniel, my heart has been broken in the best ways. He has inspired many things I've said on the radio, he inspired me to help start ministries for kids with special needs, and he helped me see God's heart more clearly. One of the greatest things Nathaniel and his family have taught me is to take whatever God gives us and to, with passion, bear fruit that helps people understand how precious and loved they are. I hope his life inspires yours as much as he has inspired me."

– Lisa Williams
Syndicated Radio Host and Coach

DEDICATION

Life can be hard, but God is faithful, every day and always. We are incredibly grateful to God for shedding His grace on us and giving us hope and a path forward after the biggest storm in our lives.

Brianna and Ashley, we cannot imagine our lives without you and are so thankful to be able to walk this journey together as a family. Nathaniel's life changed our lives and your lives forever. We know it has not always been an easy road, but we are grateful for the ways you have loved, helped, and sacrificed for your brother. Thank you for choosing to embrace the joys and pain and for allowing God to shape and use your lives through it. We love you and are so proud of you.

We will always hold an immeasurable amount of love and gratitude for all those who have loved and cared for Nathaniel and our family.

CONTENTS

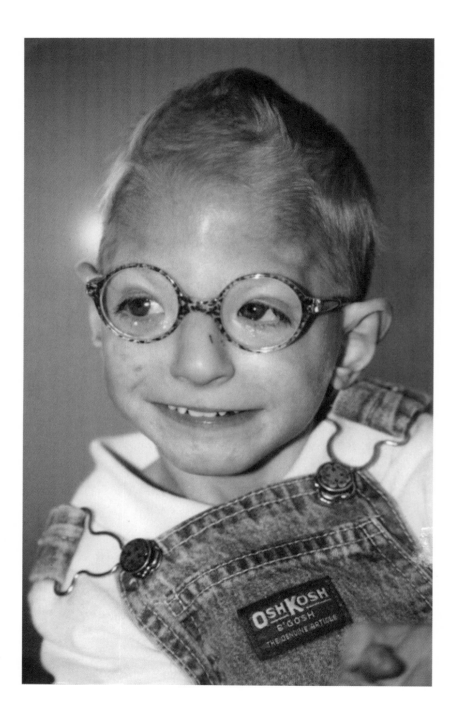

FIRST THOUGHTS

Hi, you guys. My name is Nathaniel Timothy Kuck. My name means "a treasured gift from God." I like knowing that Mom and Dad named me that because they thought of me as their treasured gift from God.

The story you are about to read is true. It's the story of my life, and it will tell you the realities of both the good times and the not-so-good times of my life. Actually, it is all good, even though it might not seem like it. A Scripture in Romans tells us: *"All things work together for good to those who love God and are called according to His purpose"* (Rom. 8:28). That's really true, but the process can be painful, you know, like exercise or running a triathlon. The process is hard, but the end result is good. After all, my story is evidence of that truth.

Mom and Dad helped me put my life story on paper. I really want to tell you my story because I want to share with you "the Hope" that my family and I have experienced. *HOPE LIVES!* Even during some of the most difficult days of pain and heartache, we found that there is always hope. Hope is an anchor that keeps you secured in a cove of peace, even in the midst of the biggest storms that life can bring. Hope is not just for my family and me; it is available to everyone!

"And now these three remain: faith, hope and love."

—1 Corinthians 13:13

That is why this book is called *Hope Lives!* It is not just my hope—"Nathaniel's Hope"—but it can be your hope, too. Cuz every life matters! So let me begin my story.

CHAPTER ONE

THE AWAKENING

"The Spirit of God has made me,
And the breath of the Almighty
gives me life."

—Job 33:4, NKJV

One day back in the fall of 1996, I kind of woke up in my mommy's tummy. I think I was about ten weeks old. I had fingers, toes, and everything! I was alive before then—it's just that I don't remember. You know how hard it is to remember everything as a kid? Well, that applies here. I was really, really cute even back then, if I do say so myself.

Mr. God (or sometimes I call him my Divine Daddy, DD), appointed my life.

Anyway, Mr. God (or sometimes I call him my Divine Daddy, DD) appointed my life. It did not just happen, but He made me for a purpose. DD says that "before I was even in my mommy's tummy, He made me!" (See Psalm 139:15–16.) He made me just like He wanted me to be. Wow! I was His creation! His masterpiece to be put on display!

I don't remember much about those early days; I was just kind of hanging out and growing, like any other kid. I remember hearing my sisters, Brianna and Ashley, giggling, playing, and sometimes even fighting with each other. They seemed to be having a lot of fun. I could hardly wait to see their smiles and to be cuddled by their hugs. It seemed like every day I would hear them pray for me while I was still in my mommy's tummy. They affectionately called me B. K., for Baby Kuck. I could tell they loved me! I always thought that was kind of neat because they hadn't even met me, yet I knew they already loved me. I had already fallen in love with my family! I could hardly wait till we could hang out together, my family and me. You know, play Uno, Scrabble, watch *Veggie Tales*, that kind of thing.

Things were going along just peachy. I was taking it easy, doing what a kid does while in his mommy's tummy—eating, sleeping, and swimming! Every once in a while, I would punch or kick my mom so she knew I was still there. I liked being the center of Mom's attention. Sometimes my dad would put his hand on my mommy's tummy, and I would kick and punch him, too! It was kinda like boxing with Dad! That was really fun. I could hardly wait till I could play with my dad all the time. He seemed like a big kid. He was the best dad ever!

One day in December 1996, I heard an unusual conversation between Mom and Dad. Not that I was eavesdropping or anything. I just don't think they knew I was listening. Dad told Mom that he felt like we were going to go through a difficult season, a time of trial. I think he called it a "season of sorrow." That didn't sound like too much fun. Mom responded quickly, wanting to know the details. Like, "Tell me more. Don't leave me hanging!" I think girls like to know everything. Anyway, Dad said it was just a sense that my Divine Daddy may have put in his heart. That was all he said. I never heard them talk about it anymore, so I didn't think too much about it.

After Christmas, in January 1997, Mom had a doctor's appointment. They used a sonogram to take a picture of me to check and see how I was doing. My first portrait! It showed I was doing fine, and the doctor even told my mom and dad that I was a boy. I think my dad wanted it to be surprise, but Mom wanted to know what kind of cute clothes to buy for me. Definitely a girl thing! Mom and Dad were really excited. Things could not have been any better.

"My frame was not hidden from you when I was made in the secret place, when I was woven together in the depths of the earth. Your eyes saw my unframed body, all the days ordained for me were written in your book, before one of them came to be." – Psalm 139: 15-16

God has a dream for each one of us. Even as are being formed, He is creating us for a purpose, and designing His plan to be woven into our DNA. Every life is important to God. Every life matters.

CHAPTER TWO

STORM WARNING

"We have this hope as an anchor for the soul, firm and secure."
—Hebrews 6:19, NIV

In May, Dad, Mom, and I went on our first big trip to Mexico to visit some missionary friends. Don't worry—I didn't drink the water! When we came back, Mom went in for another checkup and to get another picture of me. She was a little worried that she was getting out of shape. But after all, I was the third kid, and we both liked to share chocolate ice cream together. Yum! But when the nurse looked into Mommy's tummy and saw me floating around, she was concerned about the amount of fluid that was in there. Mommy's tummy was kinda bigger than it was supposed to be. I didn't mind it cuz it was like being in an Olympic-size swimming pool! I had more room to play and practice my backstroke.

But the doctor was concerned enough that he arranged for an appointment with a special doctor called a perinatologist, who helps babies who are in their mommies' tummies. (Is that a mouthful, or what? Six syllables! Most kids my age could manage only one syllable.)

My mom and dad took me to see Dr. C. He was a very nice doctor who seemed to be genuinely concerned about my mom and me. After using a special sonogram machine that could get some close-up pictures of me, he, too, was concerned that something might be not quite right. He confirmed that Mommy's tummy was too big, and

I knew that my Divine Daddy was making me, and this was not a news flash to Him. He was in control.

it wasn't just because we were eating too many scoops of ice cream! He thought I might not be swallowing and processing the amniotic fluid properly. How was I supposed to know what to do? That was the first time I had been in such a situation.

Anyway, the doc said there might be a blockage in my intestines, something called *duodenal atresia*. When I heard that, I thought, "What the heck is that?" The doc began to explain that maybe tissue had grown together and was blocking my bowel system, not letting the amniotic fluid process through my bowels and back out the umbilical cord. I did not really understand all this stuff, but I wasn't going to stress about it. I knew that my Divine Daddy was making me, and this was not a news flash to Him. He was in control.

A few more days went by, or maybe even a week, and they wanted to do another sonogram to check me out. Once again, they found that Mommy's tummy was getting really big. Dad could thump it like a watermelon. Mom did not think it was all that funny. I heard the doc say Mommy's tummy was actually bigger than if I were a full nine months old. I wasn't even seven months old yet!

When Dad asked if the doc saw anything else he was concerned about, the doc hesitated slightly and said he had some questions regarding my head, but he told Dad not to worry. I knew that really made my dad worry. I was hanging out, trying to figure out what was next, when all of sudden, I saw this big pointed thing come right through Mommy's tummy. It was real close to me! Yikes! If that thing poked me, I am pretty sure it would really hurt. I tried to listen real hard, and I heard the doc talking to my mom and dad. He said it would relieve some of the pressure to take out some amniotic fluid through a needle. Mommy was not feeling very good because her tummy was humongous (which means really big, you know, like beach-ball size). He also said he would have some of the fluid tested to see if I was okay or not.

Was I okay? What did that mean? Would my mom and dad still love me even if I wasn't "okay" or like other kids? I didn't want to disappoint them. I mean, I've overheard other parents say that they don't really care if their kid is a boy or girl, just as long as the baby is healthy. What if this wasn't part of their plan? Would they still want me? I knew they had dreams for me, but I also knew that my Divine Daddy had a special purpose for me. I did not end up here by chance. I needed to keep reminding myself of this! I was on His assignment, and that was good enough for me!

EVERY LIFE IS A GIFT

"For you formed my inward parts; you wove me in my mother's womb. I will give thanks to you, for I am fearfully and wonderfully made."
—Psalm 139:13, NAS

When God says we are made in His image, does He really mean everyone? Or does He make accidents? In God's kingdom, there are no "oops!" Every person is created with value and purpose. There are things that kids with special needs can teach us that typical kids may not...

like how to love unconditionally.

Unconditional love is love that has no limits or conditions! In 1 Corinthians 13, God tells us that to love someone unconditionally, we must make the *choice* to love unconditionally. Will you make that choice?

Love is patient, love is kind. It does not envy, it does not boast, it is not proud. It does not dishonor others, it is not self-seeking, it is not easily angered, it keeps no record of wrongs.
Love does not delight in evil but rejoices with the truth.
It always protects, always trusts, always hopes, always perseveres. Love never fails.
– 1 Corinthians 13:4-8

CHAPTER THREE

READY OR NOT

"'For I know the plans I have for you,'
declares the LORD…'plans to give you
hope and a future.'"

—Jeremiah 29:11, NIV

About two weeks after my second sonogram, my family and I were hanging at our home when the phone rang. It was a doctor, and he told Mommy that everything looked fine, chromosomes and all. Mommy started to cry and cry and cry. Why is it that when women get really good news, they cry? I don't get it! Dad, on the other hand, was like a rock; he was still very serious, concerned, and convinced that we needed to stay prepared for some challenges.

Well, a couple more weeks went by, and it was now June 4. My mom began to have cramps and contractions. They seemed to be painful! I was thinking how glad I was to be a boy, since we do not have to get pregnant and have labor pains. The doctor recommended that Mommy check into the hospital because her body was telling her it was time for me to come out and face the brave new world. The problem was, I only weighed a little over three pounds, and I was only thirty weeks old. It wasn't time for me to come yet! So Mom checked into the hospital, and the doctors gave her some medicine that would tell her body not to send me out into the world, at least not yet. They also did that needle thing again and drained my pool a little. Gee whiz, that was scary, but it made Mom feel a little better.

My Divine Daddy had handpicked a pretty special family for me.

Mom, Dad, and my sisters hung out at the hospital with me most of the time. But when Dad and my sisters went home at night, I liked hanging out with just Mom. She would talk to me, pray for me, and tell me she loved me. Pretty cool having a mom like that.

My Divine Daddy had handpicked a pretty special family for me. I knew that He had a special plan for us all. I don't think Mom and Dad knew it yet, but they were entering the classroom—and I was going to be their teacher.

"Show me your ways Lord. Teach me your paths."
– Psalm 25:4

The greatest lessons in life are not usually acquired from a text book. More often than not, God uses the mountains and valleys of life to teach us. If you are in the classroom, embrace the journey. What lessons are you learning?

CHAPTER FOUR

IT'S BEGINNING TO RAIN

"He causes his sun to rise on the evil and the good, and sends rain on the righteous and the unrighteous."
—Matthew 5:45, NIV

On June 5, at about 11:00 p.m., there was a commotion in the room. I awoke from a deep sleep. I was having a dream. I can't remember what it was, and I was probably swimming because I had not learned how to throw a football yet. I heard one of the doctors talking to Mom. He told her that they found an infection in the amniotic fluid, something like "negative gram rods," and that they were going to need to take the baby by C-section. I did not know what all that this meant, but this much I knew: I was that baby! Mom called Dad and told him. He called Grandpa and Grandma and asked them to watch my sisters.

When Dad arrived at the hospital, Mom was kind of tense, and she asked Dad if he had a peace about the delivery. He told her, "How I can possibly have peace when I receive a call at midnight about having an emergency C-section to deliver my son?" They prayed in the hospital room, which helped, I could tell. Then they wheeled Mom and me into the OR.

Dad waited until they called him in for the delivery process. Dad had called the family, so they knew, and they came to be there with us. That was a real blessing because it was 3:00 a.m. I was used to being up, but no one else was.

Mom, Dad, and I were all in the delivery room with all the doctors and nurses, of course. They gave Mom something that made her sleep. Dad was there with a video camera, ready to capture the Kodak moment of my arrival. After all, Dad and Mom had been dreaming about this day for a long time. Somehow I don't think this was in their plan, but my Divine Daddy had a different plan. From what I understood, this C-section was going to be kinda messy. Dad did not care for it too much, but he did his best to get some of it on video.

Before you knew it, I was out of Mommy's tummy. At first, it was kind of tough breathing. They cleaned me up and then put a thing over my mouth, which pushed lots of air into my lungs. My lungs had never had air before; this was a new thing for me. It was kind of hard, but I began to get the hang of this breathing thing. Dad was there, still taking video. It was the first time I saw him and he saw me. I thought he kind of looked like me, actually. I heard the doctor say I had an APGAR score of 3. I thought, "What in the world does that acronym stand for, and what does it mean? I think maybe it meant that these people thought I wasn't perfect, by their standard, but was I not perfect in the eyes of my Divine Daddy? Did He not knit my innermost parts together in my mom's belly? Was I not created in His image? How could I be anything but perfect?

I think maybe that meant that these people thought I wasn't really perfect, by their standard, but was I not perfect in the eyes of my Divine Daddy?

I would sometimes hear people talk about kids before they came into the world. As they anxiously waited, they would guess if they would have a boy or girl, although what mattered the most was that the baby was healthy...or perfect.

Would my mom and dad still love me? Would they still believe that I was their "treasured gift from God?"

I think that means I am not really perfect in the eyes of man, but I still can be perfect in the eyes of my Divine Daddy. No matter, I was on the way to a place called NICU. I know what that stands for: Neonatal Intensive Care Unit. I like the Care part of it. When I got there, they cleaned me up, and then they hooked me up to all these machines. You know what the worst part was? Them sticking a tube down my throat into my stomach and also one into my lungs to help me breathe. It made me want to gag. Think about it—how would you like someone to cram something like a garden hose down your throat? They also stuck these little circles on me with wires. The RNs (registered nurses) and the RTs (registered therapists) would watch these screens with numbers. I thought it might be like a video game or like TV; maybe they had on *Cailou,* my favorite cartoon. They were always looking at it and talking. I was kind of cranky; I had been up all night with no nap, and I was hungry. By the way, I had this straw-like thing coming out of my head; I heard them call it an IV. One of the RNs put something into the straw, and I don't remember anything else.

EVERY LIFE MATTERS

How do you respond to the news of a child being born with special needs? If we believe that every life is a gift, "I am sorry" should be replaced with the words "I am with you." Cheering on and walking the uncharted journey with someone with a child with special needs will be an immeasurable blessing. If you are on that journey, know that your child matters and is not a second-class citizen. Every life is a gift from God and matters.

CHAPTER FIVE

THE CRACK OF THUNDER

"God is our refuge and strength, an ever-present help in trouble."

—Psalm 46:1, NIV

While I was catching a few Zs, Mom and Dad were not having fun. I was not there, but this is what I heard had happened. Mom had come out of surgery and was in recovery with Dad, who was waiting for her to wake up. As she began to wake up, the anesthesiologist, Dr. H, said they wanted to observe her for an hour or two before she would be moved to a room. Dad thought it was fine and the hard part was over. A little while later, the nurses seemed a little tense, and they began to give my mom some fluid. Mom was kind of in and out of consciousness. She was really weak. At one point, my dad saw two of the nurses kind of whispering to one another while looking at the TV screen thing with the numbers. They seemed nervous, and that made my dad really nervous. That was different for Dad cuz he was the one who was supposed to be strong and in charge. He was our rock.

Sometime around 4:00 a.m., the doctor said he could not seem to get Mom's blood pressure to stabilize. They had been adding fluids and expanders, but none of that seemed to be working. He said he had ordered more blood to see if that would help her stabilize. He also said there was a possibility that she was bleeding or hemorrhaging. He went ahead and called the OB/GYN doctor and asked him to return to the hospital, just in case they needed to open Mommy back up to find out where she might be bleeding. It just so happened that on that night and at that time, the vac transport system, which is used to carry medications and blood, was not in operation. Security needed to transport the blood from the blood bank within the hospital. It seemed like forever, and the blood still was not here. The anesthesiologist said he needed to take Mom back into surgery because he was better equipped with life-support equipment there. Dad asked Uncle Duane and Auntie Pam to come in and pray for Mommy. When Mommy woke momentarily and saw all of them there praying for her, she said, "Is something wrong? Am I going to die?"

The doctors rolled Mommy back in the OR and began to operate on her. The replacement blood still had not arrived. Dad stayed right outside the OR, pacing and praying. Dad had my grandpa, uncles, and aunts call people to tell them that Mommy's life was at risk and that we needed them to pray. I was glad people were going to pray because I know that my Divine Daddy hears our prayers.

Another surgeon who was sleeping at the hospital scrubbed and went into the OR. A few minutes later, the blood finally arrived, followed by the OB/GYN. Now there was a total of five doctors and maybe eight nurses in the OR trying to save Mommy's life. At one point, a nurse came out, and Daddy asked if everything was okay. She said they were doing the best they could. The intensity increased even further. The prayers became even more intense. Another fifteen minutes passed; the other surgeon who was on call had been sleeping at the hospital, and he arrived. He asked Dad how many children they had, and Dad told them there were three. Because now there was me! The doctor said they might need to do a partial hysterectomy. Daddy said, "Whatever you have to do to save her life, please do it." The doctor hurried back into the OR, and Daddy shared the situation with our family and then went back to praying. God heard every prayer that was prayed.

It was another twenty minutes or so until the doctor came

back out and said he thought Mom had stabilized. Dad was relieved, but he still kept praying. Another thirty minutes passed, and the anesthesiologist came out and said Mommy had definitely stabilized and that it looked like she was going to be okay. He proceeded to share that there was a period of five minutes when he did not know if Mommy was going to make it or not. I know my Divine Daddy kept my mommy alive. He just used the doctors to help Him do what needed to be done. God had a purpose for my mommy. "Surely, as I have planned, so it will be, and as I have purposed, so it will happen" (Isa. 14:24). He heard every prayer that was prayed. Dad was so relieved that Mommy was going live! He knew that God had intervened. The doctor told Dad that Mom should be coming out to recovery in about thirty minutes. Dad went to the waiting room and shared the reassuring news.

> *"Surely, as I have planned, so it will be, and as I have purposed, so it will happen."*
> *—Isaiah 14:24*

During that critical day, many who knew nothing about what was wrong were burdened to pray. Miss Shirley, Mom's dear friend (and a woman who really knows how to pray), had a burden to pray for Mom and me all day! She cried out to God for us without even knowing the urgency of the matter.

During the night, Divine Daddy woke many people up to pray, even before they knew this was kind of a life-and-death thing. In fact, my Grandpastor Rich actually woke up one night after having a dream that someone was trying to kill my mom, and he immediately began to pray.

From that point on, I understood the power of prayer. I was thankful that these people listened and stood in the gap for us. They were faithful to pray when we needed it most. Those prayers made such a difference! That is the best way anyone could help us! Cuz prayer works!

DOES GOD HEAR OUR PRAYERS?

"And in the same way—by our faith—the Holy Spirit helps us with our daily problems and in our praying. For we don't even know what we should pray for nor how to pray as we should, but the Holy Spirit prays for us with such feeling that it cannot be expressed in words."
—*Romans 8:26, TLB*

Not only does God hear our prayers, but He helps us when we are at a loss for words. When our hearts are aching over the challenges we face, or those who have lost loved ones, God knows, understands, and will act in response to our prayers. The Holy Spirit hears our cries of desperation, tears, and other expressions of our hearts and moves on our behalf. Just like earthly parents want to help their children, our Heavenly Father does also, but even so much more so. Tell God the things that concern you. He is listening.

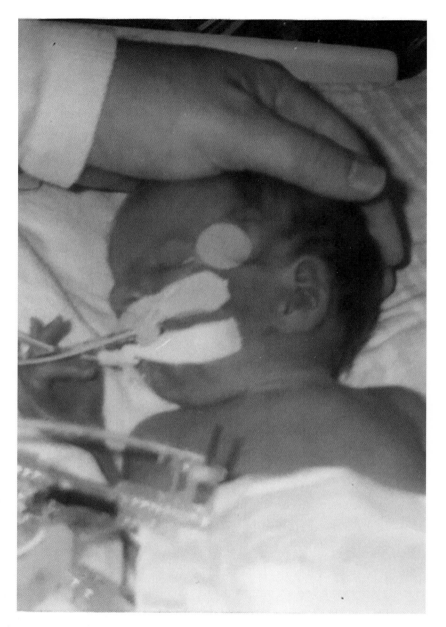

Nathaniel spent his first eighty-nine days in the NICU.
(Neonatal Intensive Care Unit)

CHAPTER SIX

THE STORM NOW PASSED

"It shall come to pass in the day that the LORD gives you rest from your sorrow, and from your fear..."

—Isaiah 14:3, NKJV

Mom finally came out of recovery. She was really hydrated (which means full of fluid and kinda big) and kind of groggy, but she recognized Daddy. It looked like everything was going to be okay. The doctor said it would take a couple of days or more in the hospital for Mom to recover.

In the meantime, Mommy really wanted to see me; after all she had not yet been able to see her one and only son. I was lying in the NICU (Neonatal Intensive Care Unit), and she was lying in the recovery room. I really wanted to see Mommy, and I knew she really wanted to see me, but I would have to wait. Daddy came to see me, but I was kind of sedated, so I really did not remember much.

Sometime the next day, Mom came down to see me in a wheelchair. They practically had to cut her tummy in half to take me out, so she couldn't walk. I was so excited when Mommy came to see me! When I heard her voice, I knew who she was; it was the same voice I had heard for nearly eight months before I was born. I heard Mom and Dad's voices, and I felt their touch. I felt such comfort! Then I heard them pray for me, and that brought me comfort also. I knew that my Divine Daddy heard their prayers, and even though I did not know the assignment God had for me, I know He had determined that my life did not just happen by chance — it was intentional, and it had purpose.

I have to admit, it was no fun being in the hospital. Day after day, Mom and Dad would sit with me in the NICU, and even my sisters came to visit. They sang to me and prayed with me.

I don't think this was what any of us ever expected or wanted. No one ever really prepared my family for this situation.

They weren't ready to be a part of this unknown community of special needs that I was bringing them into. It just wasn't part of their plan. I hoped that after they got over their early disappointment, they would learn to love me and accept me. I guess it can be kinda tough for parents to accept a plan they didn't choose. I know they wished I could be like everyone else, but I am not. I am not perfect by the world's standards, but I am who God made me. I am a VIP—a kid with Value and Incredible Purpose—and God has a plan for me. I am okay with that.

I think it was really hard for Mom and Dad when people would feel sorry for them. Was I something to be pitied? I mean, I know I wasn't perfect, but I was still a kid that God made! I was Mom and Dad's kid! They were trying to embrace their new life with me, and what they really needed was friends who would walk this journey with them. They didn't need to have people try to give them all the answers or try to fix anything. Why do people always think they have to do that? They just needed a little encouragement. You know, a little encouragement can go a long way! Truett Cathy (founder of Chick-fil-A) once said, "How do you know if someone needs encouragement? If they are breathing."

After ten days, I was prepared to go into surgery. I was still on the ventilator, which helped me breathe, and they had given me an IV called a "central line" because it flowed into a large artery near my heart. I still had the tube down my stomach and the sticky things with wires to monitor my heart. There was even something strapped to my leg to measure my blood pressure and a little Velcro thing (called an oximeter) that measured the oxygen level in my blood.

On one hand, I was looking forward to surgery so maybe I could get unhooked from some of the machines. On the other hand, I knew my mom and dad were really worried. They prayed with the doctors and nurses before the operation. Again, I knew that my Divine Daddy had heard those prayers. I could tell by the sound of Mom and Dad's voices that they were concerned. I wanted so much to tell them not to worry, that God would take care of things, and I would be okay. I *knew* He had sent me here for a reason.

A couple of hours later, they rolled me back into the NICU. Mom and Dad were waiting for me. I was groggy, and my tummy hurt. After the surgery, the doctor told Mom and Dad that they found a blockage in my intestine and fixed it. My parents were really happy. Now all I needed to do was heal, get off the machines, and begin to eat. I could hardly wait!

What is it like to learn that your family's plans have changed when you have been blessed with a child with special needs? Emily Perl Kingsley is an American wirter who joined the *Sesame Street* team in 1970. Her son Jason was born with Down syndrome changed her life. She shares a valuable perspective about when life sends you a detour.

WELCOME TO HOLLAND

I am often asked to describe the experience of raising a child with a disability—to try to help people who have not shared that unique experience to understand it, to imagine how it would feel. It's like this…

When you're going to have a baby, it's like planning a fabulous vacation trip—to Italy. You buy a bunch of guidebooks and make your wonderful plans. The Coliseum. The Michelangelo David. The gondolas in Venice. You may learn some handy phrases in Italian. It's all very exciting.

After months of eager anticipation, the day finally arrives. You pack your bags and off you go. Several hours later, the plane lands. The stewardess comes in and says, "Welcome to Holland."

"Holland?!?" you say. "What do you mean Holland?? I signed up for Italy! I'm supposed to be in Italy. All my life I've dreamed of going to Italy."

But there's been a change in the flight plan. They've landed in Holland, and there you must stay.

The important thing is that they haven't taken you to a horrible, disgusting, filthy place full of pestilence, famine ,and disease. It's just a different place.

So you must go out and buy new guidebooks. And you must learn a whole new language. And you will meet a whole new group of people you would never have met.

It's just a different place. It's slower-paced than Italy, less flashy than Italy. But after you've been there for a while and you catch your breath, you look around…and you begin to notice that Holland has windmills…and Holland has tulips. Holland even has Rembrandts.

But everyone you know is busy coming and going from Italy…and they're all bragging about what a wonderful time they had there. And for the rest of your life, you will say, "Yes, that's where I was supposed to go. That's what I had planned."

And the pain of that will never, ever, ever, ever go away—because the loss of that dream is a very, very significant loss.

But…if you spend your life mourning the fact that you didn't get to Italy, you may never be free to enjoy the very special, the very lovely things…about Holland.[1]

2. Emily Perl Kingsley, "Welcome to Holland," c. 1987. All rights reserved. ADD PERMISSION WHEN OBTAINED.

Our first family photo

CHAPTER SEVEN

DON'T WASTE YOUR SORROWS

"Not only so, but we also glory in our sufferings, because we know that suffering produces perseverance; perseverance, character; and character, hope."
—Romans 5:3–4, NIV

Whether we like it or not, suffering seems to be a part of every life. I know my mom and dad don't like it, but it is often where their greatest dependency on God is found. Dad says, "Life is hard, but God is faithful." This really neat lady, Joni Eareckson Tada, writes, "Heartache forces us to embrace God out of desperate, urgent need. God is never closer than when your heart is aching." She also says, "The faintest prayers of those who suffer reach more deeply into God's heart." My Divine Daddy must have known what He was doing when He allowed suffering to be designed into life.

Well, a couple of weeks had now passed, and we had a really big day. Mom and Dad held me for the very first time. It was awesome! I always wondered what it would be like to have Mom and Dad hold me. My eyesight was not really that good, but I could look into my mom and dad's eyes. It was even better than I thought. About the same time, I was taken off the ventilator, and I was breathing on my own with the help of some oxygen. That was way cool.

I even was beginning to eat on my own. It wasn't steak and potatoes, mind you, but it was sure better than always being hungry. I was learning to take a bottle and suck, swallow, and breathe. Most of my food still came with the tube down my throat, which let gravity do its thing. The bad thing about that is, where is the fun in eating? No savoring the food or tantalizing your taste buds—you know what I mean.

I was starting to get the hang of it, and then I took a couple of steps backward. I don't know why, but something was not right. I kept having a tummy ache that didn't go away! My stomach wasn't processing food properly. I kept throwing up

(Dad says, "calling Earl") whatever they would give me. Just as I was beginning to chunk on the weight, now I was losing weight. This was not good because I weighed only about three pounds, six ounces.

After a week or so of not being able to eat, they had to begin to feed me through an IV. They also did a GI test, which revealed that my intestines just were not working. I definitely wouldn't classify any of this as fun. The worst part was seeing how worried Mom and Dad would get. One of the best parts was that I had made a lot of friends in NICU; they were taking care of me to the best of their ability. I really like being loved on, especially by the caregivers who engaged their hearts as well as their hands. I could tell the difference between those who really cared and those who were there because they had to be. I had a real special nurse named Jill who was always my primary caregiver when she was on duty. She was really sweet; she called me her "love bug."

> *I really like being loved on, especially by the caregivers who engaged their hearts as well as their hands.*

After a couple of weeks of not eating, Auntie Jill (that's what I called her because she is like family) got really upset. She sought out one of the doctors and sat him down. She began to tell him that something was wrong and that he needed to do surgery to find out what it might be. She even cried some while telling him. She really cared for me, and I think she even loved me.

The doctors did not think anything was wrong with my gut, but they were willing to consider surgery. Mom and Dad could not bear to think of another significant surgery, but they did not really have a choice. They knew they had to do something. After speaking with the doctors, they set a date of August 7 for the surgery. It was my sister's birthday. I was already two months old, but I weighed only three and a half pounds. I was still very sick. I already had this really big scar across my belly from the previous surgery, so they were going to cut me in the same spot. Unfortunately the scar is above my bathing-suit line; what will people think when I am older, basking in the sun, catching a few rays? I figured I would tell them I took a bullet or a bayonet when I was in the army or something. I wanted to think of something that sounds kind of macho because I was such a handsome hunk.

I did not remember much, but I do remember Mom and Dad walking beside me as they rolled me down to the operating room again. I think I remember Mom and Dad praying with the doctors and nurses, and that was about it. Boy, when I woke up, did my tummy hurt. It was like I had a zipper from one side of my tummy to the other. Good thing I did not have to bend over and tie my shoes. Matter of fact, I did not even have any shoes or know what they were. The surgeon told Mom and Dad that he found an area of my colon that was abscessed, so they had to remove about four inches of bowel. He was very surprised but thankful that they found out what was wrong.

After a few days, I was kind of getting back to normal— well, what was normal for me. I had not begun to eat yet, but everyone was hopeful. Mom and Dad wanted so much that I could eat and process food. Finally, after about a week, they said I could begin to take food through my stomach. They fed me through a tube down my mouth, and my intestines began to work. Now the fun really began! Just think, before long, I'll be chomping down baby-back ribs and ice cream sundaes. Yummy!

It is now the third week of August, and I am really chunking on the weight and starting to feel much better. There is even talk about me going home soon. The problem is, I am still not able to eat with my mouth, so they said I needed to get something called a G-tube. They will cut a hole in my stomach and insert a tube so my food will go directly into my stomach by something called gravity. I do not know what gravity is because I have not even been to kindergarten yet, but it worked. The good news is that I won't be as hungry anymore; the bad news is that baby-back ribs won't fit down the tube. It is all formula. Not that I want to sound ungrateful, but that formula can be kind of nasty. But I will get used to it, by the grace of God. Oh yeah, one last important thing: I somehow got a double hernia—go figure! How in the world did I get a hernia lying in my crib? I never tried to move the furniture or anything. Actually, they said I might have gotten it by crying. Were they suggesting I was a crybaby?

Though my mom and dad were disappointed again, they knew they had to cross this road if they were going to take me home. Once again, on August 30, I was rolled into surgery. The great news is, I quickly recovered, and the doctors and nurses were hoping to let me go home by my mom's birthday, on August 31. The big day finally came, and I was going home. It was August 30. Dad and Mom were so happy! I couldn't figure it out. Dad was so happy, but he couldn't stop crying. I am not a grown-up or anything, but when I'm happy, I'm gonna laugh, not cry. I was now a handsome, four-pound hunk, ready to break out of the hospital. Hot dog!

THE PURPOSE OF PAIN AND SUFFERING

"My grace is sufficient for you,
for my power is made perfect in weakness."
—2 Corinthians 12:9, NIV

A diving accident in 1967 left Joni Eareckson Tada a quadriplegic in a wheelchair, unable to use her hands. Through her own journey of pain and suffering she found hope and a deep desire to share this with others resulting in the establishment of Joni and Friends, an international Christian organization advancing disability ministry around the world (www.joniandfriends.org). In the "Beyond Suffering" bible, she shares this commentary that helps us see God's purpose for pain and suffering:

In today's culture of comfort and instant gratification, there is no patience for suffering. Yet suffering may well be God's choicest tool in shaping the character of Christ in us. God tells us that weakness is the secret of strength and success. It is not that weakness is merely a prerequisite for God's power; they exist simultaneously when a wounded, broken heart stops asking "Why?" with a clenched fist and starts asking "Why?" with a searching heart. Divine power washes away discouragement when a bruised and battered soul simply looks Godward.[1]

We live in a culture of death that believes that a person is better off dead than disabled. But as we allow God to fill us with hope, we can help others see that life is worth living. Where we see despair, we can offer hope. It's about passing on the hope. We can become a blessing to others through discovering God's gift of hope for our own brokenness.

---

3. Joni Eareckson Tada, *Beyond Suffering Bible* (Carol Stream, Illinois: Tyndale House Publishers, 2016), A8–A15.

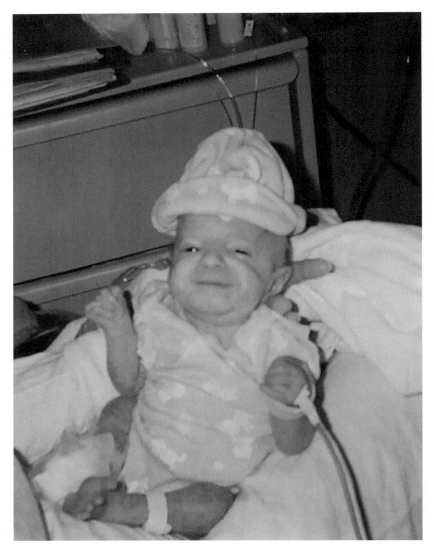

Going Home!

CHAPTER EIGHT

CHECKOUT TIME

"I thank my God every time
I remember you."
—Philippians 1:3, NIV

I was so grateful for my caregivers at Arnold Palmer Hospital that I wanted to let them know. I had my mom and dad write my most special nurse, Auntie Jill, a letter. I figured I could write the others later, but I wanted Auntie Jill to know now how much I appreciated her unconditional love.

From Nathaniel's Crib...
August 30, 1997

Dear Auntie Jill,

It has now been eighty-six days since I came into this world. (It is hard to believe that I am only three months old, and already I can almost count to a hundred. I must be smart like my dad!) My first few months of life have been so hard. There seemed to be so much pain and suffering. Not just physically, but also emotionally. I saw so many people in my family by my bedside. I could see the pain on their faces. Especially Mom and Dad. They were being torn apart as they watched me fight for life. I knew that they had entrusted my life to God, but still, there was sorrow and suffering. I heard my dad say that the "soil of suffering is fertile, and it produces maturity and growth if we let God work in us as we walk through times of suffering." Mom said, "You either become bitter or better." I don't know what all that means, but Mom and Dad seemed to believe what they were saying, and they seemed to draw comfort each time they bowed their heads to pray.

During my eighty-six days, your hands touched me and comforted me more than anyone else's, including my mom's and dad's. I always knew your caring touch. Even though I was often in a lot of pain, you were there because you knew what I liked. You knew how to put me to sleep and how to position me just right, and I loved snuggling up to the precious little lamb you gave me—a Beanie Baby nonetheless! Sometimes you even sang to me. I really liked that because your kind, caring voice brought me rest.

Your primary job was to care for me, but I wanted to thank you for caring for my mom and dad. They really needed your caring hands and hearts also. You brought peace and comfort to them because they had total confidence in you as you cared for me. I think the Sovereign Lord brought us together during this difficult time. It seems that as I reflect back over all the times your hands were on me, I could almost see the healing hands of Jesus holding yours. I saw how God used you to convince the doctors to operate on me to bring me healing.

> *You brought peace and comfort to them because they had complete confidence in you as you cared for me.*

It is true that I still have a long road ahead, and it will likely be hard at times, but God is always faithful. After all, He is the One who gives me my every breath.

I know we will always be friends because we are now family. Just remember, you can choose your friends, but you can't choose your relatives. I will be forever grateful for the love you have shown me, and I will always love you because you first loved me. Thank you for giving of yourself, not just your talent. Your caring made a difference in my life and my family's. You are a blessing.

Your Love Bug,
Nathaniel Timothy Kuck

COMPASSIONATE CAREGIVERS

"So we cared for you. Because we loved you so much,
we were delighted to share with you not only the
gospel of God but our lives as well."
—1 Thessalonians 2:8, NIV

Those who care for kids in critical care play an important role in the lives of these families who have been thrust into a community they have not been prepared for. Often, well-meaning family and friends cannot understand the intensity of the situation or the roller-coaster journey. The compassionate hearts and hands of medical caregivers not only bring life to the patient, but often nurture the souls of the weary parents. Medical caregivers are in a place to deliver either a message of hope or despair. Caregivers must walk the fine line of speaking truth without delivering a devastating blow that will rob a family of hope. Living the daily reality without losing hope can be a challenge, but no matter how bleak a situation may look, no one really knows the outcome. Choose to hang on to hope!

CHAPTER NINE

"THERE'S NO PLACE LIKE HOME"

Dorothy, *The Wizard of Oz*

It was great being home for Mom's birthday. Mom said it was the best birthday present she has ever had, even though I came home on oxygen, hooked up to a heart monitor and IV. Mom and Dad were so happy, and so was I. You know what they say: home is where your heart is. And my heart was here.

I was settling into my life at home. I had twenty-four-hour care; sometimes nurses helped, but Mom was always there. She gave everything to take care of me. She slept on the floor in the nursery all night long (or as much as I would let her), night after night. I knew this was really hard on her, but she would have it no other way. Mom and Dad had to learn how to take care of me. They had to learn how to use the G-tube, heart monitor, SAT monitor, and even set up IVs.

Mom and Dad had to learn how to take care of me.

I remember the first time my G-tube popped out. Dad had stayed home with me for some manly bonding time while Mom went to church with my sisters. Dad was sitting there lovingly holding me, and as I shifted, it popped. All of a sudden, Dad felt warm liquid all over his stomach. Now, Dad only knew of a couple of warm liquids, but this time, it was my stomach contents. There he was, home alone with me, when a hole in my tummy the size of Dad's thumb drained out all that nasty formula. Dad totally freaked out. He called Mom on her cell phone. She came home right away, and they took me to the hospital. The G-tube was placed back in my tummy, and we all returned home. What a relief; I was just starting to get hungry, and when I get hungry, I get cranky, if you know what I mean.

Well, after a couple more times of going to the hospital and having a resident install my feeding tube, Mom and Dad learned how to put it back in themselves. They had now earned the status of RPs—Registered Parents.

Fall was now here, and on October 22, something really cool happened. My "little big" sister Ashley, who was then three years old, told Mom and Dad she wanted to know Jesus. It was so cool that she wanted Jesus to be a part of her life. That night, she prayed and asked Jesus to forgive her of her sins and invited Jesus into her heart. This was encouraged by my big sis Brianna. I was in the room right next door, but I knew what was happening, and I was so excited that I wanted to jump up and dance! Of course I couldn't even walk, let alone dance, but I wanted to.

A few days later, when Mom and Dad were praying with my sisters before bedtime, Ashley told Mom and Dad that I was going to go back in the hospital. My parents told Ashley not to say that. They thought Ashley was saying that because she was jealous of all the time Mom and Dad spent with me.

The next night—I think it was a Sunday—Ashley said it again. Mom and Dad once again told her not to talk that way. My mom and dad could not bear to think of me going back into the hospital.

I had now been home almost two months, and I was starting to get sick. This was not good because I still was on oxygen, and I had a cold that had moved into my lungs. I began to struggle with my breathing. Mom and Dad took me to the kids' doctor (pediatrician). He was not sure he could treat my condition, so he sent us to a doctor who helps people breathe better, a pulmonologist. He took X-rays and found that I had the possibility of pneumonia in one of my lungs. He also told Mom and Dad some other really bad news.

THE UNEXPECTED STORMS OF LIFE

"When you pass through the waters,
I will be with you;
and when you pass through the rivers,
they will not sweep over you.
When you walk through the fire,
you will not be burned;
the flames will not set you ablaze."
—Isaiah 43:2, NIV

When we find ourselves smack dab in the middle of one of life's unexpected storms, it's encouraging to remember God's promise in Hebrews 13:5 that He will never leave us or forsake us. In fact, when we are in the valley, He will often carry us through the storms of life that surround us. When you are tempted to think that God has left you to deal with your problems all alone, think again. You are not alone. Don't lose hope! Hang on even when you don't feel like it. Tie a knot in the rope, and just hang on to hope!

> *"Weeping may last through the night,*
> *but joy comes with the morning."*
> *—Psalm 30:5, NLT*

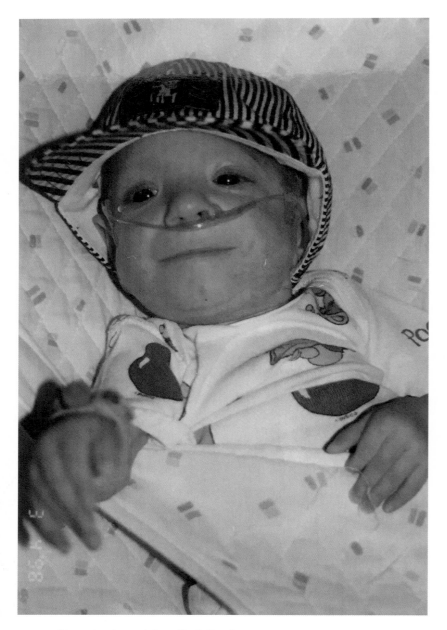

Even in the midst of trials, there were many treasures.
Our "little man" brought us great joy!

CHAPTER TEN

COUNT IT ALL JOY

"Consider it pure joy, my brothers and sisters, whenever you face trials of many kinds, because you know that the testing of your faith produces perseverance. Let perseverance finish its work so that you may be mature and complete, not lacking anything."

—James 1:2–4, NIV

The doctor saw on my X-ray that I had cracked ribs. I knew I had been fussy and tender, but I don't like to be called a crybaby. I couldn't tell Mom and Dad what was wrong; actually, I wasn't sure myself. The doctor told us that my ribs were already healing and that it was not a fresh break, but it had happened some time ago. Mom and Dad were upset and confused. They had no idea how or when it could have happened. After all, it wasn't like I was in the backyard playing tackle football. They were comforted to know that the fractures were well on the way to being healed, but confused and perplexed as to how this could have happened.

The really disturbing news was that the doctor had to report us to the Child Protection Team at the hospital and also to the HRS (I think they call it the Department of Children and Families now). Mom and Dad were shaken up but thought it was an appropriate protocol and figured it would be just fine. The doctor had discussed with them the possiblity of keeping me in the hospital overnight, but Mom and Dad pleaded with him to let us go home. He finally let me go home. I was really happy about that.

About an hour after we got home, Child Services was at the front door. A case worker had come to check out what kind of parenting and home life I had. Specifically, they wanted to know if my mom and dad had hurt me. I wasn't able to communicate, so I couldn't tell them that Mom and Dad would never hurt me. They did talk to my sisters and asked how they were disciplined and stuff like that. Actually, the case worker was very nice and just doing her job; she did not see a problem, and she called her supervisor. Her supervisor wanted to know if I should be taken away from Mom and Dad to protect me. She said that would not be necessary, but the supervisor was not convinced. Finally, it was decided that I could stay the night at home, but we would need to go to the hospital the next day for further evaluation.

I was happy about that because I knew no one loved me like my mom and dad, and no one was going to care for me like them. I still had all the contraptions—heart monitor, oxygen, SAT monitor, and nebulizer. It was really hard to roll over and get comfy at night, if you know what I mean. I could not bear the thought of being back in the hospital.

The next day, we went back to the hospital, where it was determined that I needed to be readmitted. What a bummer! I wanted to cry. Matter of fact, I think I did, and I know Mom and Dad did, too. The primary reason I had to stay in the hospital was to be in a place where I could be monitored and it could be determined whether or not my parents were hurting me. Mom and Dad were devastated and brokenhearted. After fighting for my life for three months in the hospital, and then twenty-four hours a day at home, someone who does not even know our family was talking about taking me away. Someone who has never met Mom and Dad, or, for that matter any of us, but was passing judgment about who should provide me life-giving care. I know I am just a kid, but something seems wrong with this picture.

Mom stayed in the hospital with me, and Dad took my sisters home. On the way home, Dad asked Ashley why she had told us a few days earlier that I was going back in the hospital. Ashley, sitting in the backseat, quickly responded (three-year-olds don't really think much before they speak anyway), "Jesus told me to tell you." Wow! Jesus told Dad that tough things

Jesus told Dad that tough things were ahead before they happened, so Dad could be reassured that my Divine Daddy had everything in control.

were ahead before they happened, so Dad could be reassured that my Divine Daddy had everything under control. That is just like my Divine Daddy. He always has a plan, and He is always there. I knew that, and I am so glad He reassured Dad. Dad knew it was my Divine Daddy, not Ashley, who told him. He just knew it. He was at peace, even in the midst of a storm.

Without going into too much detail, let me tell you about what turned out to be a few of Mom and Dad's most difficult weeks. Mom and Dad literally had to fight to keep me in their care. My dad ended up getting two attorneys, but some people were still talking about taking me away from my parents. Detectives came to the hospital and to the house to ask questions, trying to determine whether or not my parents were fit to care for me. I wanted to scream! Of course they are; they did not break my ribs or shake me out of anger. My dad and mom had asked our pediatrician, pediatric surgeon, neonatologist, RTs, RNs, and home health care nurses to testify if necessary. They all said they would. Our pediatrician even contacted the doctor who was heading up the Child Protection Team to tell him that Mom and Dad were great parents and that they were wrong about them abusing me. The doctor responded by saying that he had heard good things about Mom and Dad, but he didn't want to meet them because it might cloud his judgment. Go figure—doesn't character count for something? Everyone was willing to stand up for Mom and Dad, but that didn't matter! Someone who had not ever met me or my mom and dad was going to decide if my parents could still care for me.

Finally Mom and Dad were okayed to keep me and care for me. It came down to the last minute and knowing the right attorney to communicate properly to clear the accusations. This was a painful experience for Mom and Dad—and one they will never forget. Mom and Dad felt violated and emotionally abused.

This season contained the good, the bad, and the ugly—you know, like that Clint Eastwood movie. The good thing is that Mom and Dad were connected with one of the best pediatricians on the planet. His name was Dr. D, and he was the best because his entire medical practice was focused on kids in need of special care, those who Mom and Dad like to call "VIP kids." Dr. D really, really cared. He believed in me and believed I was worth a lot and worth saving. He even prayed for me!

The bad thing was that not everyone was like Dr. D. While we were in the hospital and when I was having trouble breathing, one of the doctors told Mom that she should sign a DNR. There we go again, another acronym; this one meant "Do Not Resuscitate." Mom was really upset and called Dad, crying. No one had ever suggested anything like that before, that my life was not worth saving! This doctor never even asked to meet with Dad; he just dropped this bomb on Mom. Dad was upset and immediately came to the hospital. Mom and Dad chose to change doctors and refused to sign a form giving the hospital permission to not try to save my life.

The ugly thing is the realization that some people, even physicians, do not place the appropriate value on life, especially when it is laden with problems like mine. I am not really that smart. Come to think of it, I have not even gone to kindergarten yet, but I know life and creation are ultimately controlled by my Divine Daddy, not by man. There is an appointed time to be born and to die. I do not understand all of this, but I do know that God created life. It is valuable and precious. You know what they say: "God doesn't make junk."

I was back home, and I was healing once again, and then came Christmas. Wouldn't you know it? My first Christmas out of my mommy's womb, and I get sick and have to go to the hospital. Mom and Dad woke up my sisters to open our presents quickly because they knew that they had to take me to the hospital. Sure enough, I was admitted. It seemed like it was always something. It is hard to share the joy of Christmas when you are in a cold, lonely hospital room, where no wants to be on Christmas Day. Nobody wanted to be there—not even me.

GOD USES ALL THINGS FOR GOOD

*"Praise be to the God and Father of our Lord Jesus Christ, the
Father of compassion and the God of all comfort, who comforts us in
all our troubles so that we can comfort those in any trouble with the
comfort we ourselves receive."*
—2 Corinthians 1:3-4, NIV

Though spending Nathaniel's first Christmas in the hospital
was not what anyone wanted to do, God used it to show the
Kucks that they were not alone. There were many others just like
them—patients, families, and caregivers—who felt the sadness
and isolation of spending this special holiday in the hospital
alone. As a result, a new tradition was birthed: *Caroling for Kids.*
Since 1998, thousands of people have joined caroling teams,
sharing hope and encouragement with patients, families, and
caregivers at children's hospitals on Christmas Day.

God can turn our hardships and pain into blessings to others
if we allow Him.

Thankful for our first Christmas together.

CHAPTER ELEVEN

GIVING THANKS

"Give thanks in all circumstances; for this is God's will for you in Christ Jesus."

—1 Thessalonians 5:18, NIV

Oh, yeah—I told you that I wanted to thank all my caregivers at Arnold Palmer Hospital. Here is the letter I wrote to them; of course I did ask my mom and dad to proofread it for me.

From Nathaniel's Crib...

To all my loving caregivers in Neo I and Neo II...

Can you believe it! It has been almost four months since I hung out with you guys in the unit. My mom and dad say that time flies if you're having fun, and if you're not having fun, it is like taking a bus. What is a Greyhound anyway? It may not all be fun, but it is great to be home. I like my room and the affection I get from my parents and my older sisters. My sister, Brianna, really likes to mother me, and Ashley likes to sing to me. She makes up her own songs, but they seem to come from her heart. I think they really love me and are really happy I am finally home after spending eighty-six days in Neo Hilton. It was all you loving caregivers there who made my bed, bathed me, fed me, and even changed my diapers. What service! You waited on me hand and foot (including those times when you would poke me in the hand and then in my foot—ouch)! I knew you were always doing what was best for me, even if it hurt.

Sometimes I felt like I was in a fishbowl. (I haven't seen a fish or a fishbowl, but I heard someone say it this one time, and I thought it was worth repeating.) It seemed like twice a day, a group of people would kind of hover over me and talk about how I was doing. I got such an education at such an early age. You know what they say: an acronym a day will keep the doctor away. There seemed to be an acronym for everything—I was on an NPO diet (you try that to keep your girlish figure—it's not my idea of fun), there were RTs, RNs, LPNs, OTs, and PTs, and don't forget MDs. Most of the time, I was HAB, which means "hungry as a bear." The people I love the most are my very own RPs, which stands for "Registered Parents." I usually just refer to them as Mom and Dad.

I knew you were all professionals and trained at providing the best care, but the thing that meant the most to me was not your hands, but your hearts. It was your caring hearts that comforted me when I was hurting. When I was fussy and inconsolable (my mom tells me I was that way a lot), it meant so much when you cared enough to take time to love on me and coddle me when I was crying. My mom and dad wanted to give me the love I needed, but they could not always be there. I missed them, but I was comforted knowing you were there when they weren't. Thank you for engaging your hearts as well as your hands. Your hearts brought as much healing to me as your hands.

> *I knew you were all professionals and trained at providing the best care, but the thing that meant the most to me was not your hands, but your hearts. It was your caring hearts that comforted me when I was hurting.*

I am six months old now and weigh nearly nine pounds. I have love handles like my dad. I know there are still things in my body that may not work perfectly, but Mom and Dad still think I'm kind of special. My dad has said, "Life is a gift; we should live it with thanks," and he says God really does not care about the stature of man, but He cares about the heart. I think God has given me a pretty good heart. Life sometimes can make our hearts hard, but God can always make them soft again.

Thank you for being willing to care for me with your hands, but especially your hearts.

I will be forever grateful,
Nathaniel Timothy Kuck

CHAPTER TWELVE

NEVER GIVE UP

"I can do all things through Christ who strengthens me."

—Philippians 4:13, NKJV

After Christmas, I ended up getting pneumonia twice—once in January and again in March. That was a big bummer. By then, I had accumulated more than 110 days in the hospital. Too bad I could not accumulate frequent-flier points for each visit. That was almost half my life. Just driving by the hospital with Mom would give me the willies.

Taking care of me was a lot of work, but I was worth it! It was hard for Mom and Dad to care for me and still give my sisters everything they needed and just manage life!

I am thankful for some special people God brought to our family to help us. It kind of took a village to care for me. Miss Diane, Miss Lynn, and Miss Sandy would sometimes come over and just hold me or help Mom carry my oxygen tanks to the doctor's office. I had a lot of stuff that had to go with me wherever I went. Sometimes I would see Mr. Ray come stand outside my bedroom window to talk

I am thankful for some special people God brought to our family to help us.

to Daddy God about me. Wow! Pastor Chris and Miss Debbie always let us know that they cared, and they were with us on our hardest days. Kari became my adopted older sister. She would come over in the afternoon and give me my breathing treatments so Mom could do other Mom things like laundry. Sometimes she would sit with me in the car in the parking lot with a walkie-talkie so Mom could do something normal, like grocery-shop.

Our life was anything but normal, but we tried to survive the best we could, in our "normal."

Oh, yeah, did I tell you I had my first birthday party on June 6? It was a lot of fun; Mom really wanted me to feel special, and I did. All my friends (mostly nurses and therapists) came. It's fun to do something like a "normal" kid.

During that same time, Mom and Dad, along with some of the doctors, were concerned about my head growth. They thought I might have something called *craniosynistosis*. This is when the bones in your head grow together before they are supposed to, which limits the growth of your brain. Is that why some people are called boneheads? I hope people do not call me a bonehead. Mom and Dad were really concerned about my head, and they sought a second opinion from a doctor at Shands Hospital in Gainesville, Florida. My parents were learning something I already knew: that men can become great doctors, but my Divine Daddy does the healing. Mom and Dad were thankful for all of man's wisdom, but they wanted to make sure they did the right thing. They prayed and prayed about what to do, and they decided to go ahead with the surgery the doctors said I needed.

ASK GOD FOR WISDOM

"If any of you lacks wisdom, you should ask God,
who gives generously to all without finding fault,
and it will be given to you."
—James 1:5, NIV

As a parent, it's often hard to know what the right thing is to do. Even within the medical field, there are conflicting opinions about the way to manage your child's care. At those crossroads of decision, we can know that God will give you wisdom as you do your best to help your child. A parent knows his or her child best and is that little one's greatest advocate! Being a parent is hard. Being a parent to a child with extra needs is extra hard. But it can also be very rewarding. So when you aren't sure what to do next, ask God for wisdom. With His help, you will find the answers you need—and the great rewards.

God gives parents good instincts, and sometimes you have to go with your gut and a prayer.

CHAPTER THIRTEEN

A TIME FOR EVERYTHING

*"To everything there is a season,
A time for every purpose under heaven."*
—Ecclesiastes 3:1, NKJV

In early June, I was once again forced to make a reservation at the Hospital Hilton for surgery. The surgery would be performed in Orlando by a neurosurgeon at Arnold Palmer Hospital. I was happy about that because I knew that a lot of people at APH loved me. I think Mom and Dad were pleased about that also. Everything went kind of okay with the surgery. I say "kind of" because after the surgery in ICU, I was bleeding so much from the incision in my head that I "coded" (hospital talk to say that I died, and they had to resuscitate me). It's a good thing Mom and Dad never signed that DNR! Everything turned out okay, but Mom was really shaken up because she was there when all of this happened.

After about four days in the hospital, I went home to heal. I heal best at home; it is kind of hard to heal in the hospital sometimes. Mom and Dad thought that after I healed, I became more responsive, and they were so hopeful that I would begin to eat with my mouth, but I just couldn't manage to do it. I would watch my sisters eat ice cream and cake, and I would begin to drool just thinking about it. The truth of the matter is that for the first few years of my life, I drooled a whole bunch.

Ever since I was born, my mom and dad have been asking my Divine Daddy for healing for my body. I wanted it, too, but I have been thinking that Divine Daddy had a bigger plan and purpose—one that I did not understand, and neither did Mom and Dad. I heard them surrender the circumstances time and time again while talking to my Divine Daddy in prayer. I think He is glorified through the act of surrender. I knew that my Divine Daddy had a really, really *big* plan because He allowed me to be born with all of my challenges. I kind of think He wanted my mom and dad to know Him in a whole different way—a way that cultivated a deeper dependency and greater maturity. Whatever that means.

During that time, I went a whole year without being in the hospital. You know that saying: it's a nice place to visit, but I wouldn't want to live there. The truth of the matter is, it's not even a nice place to visit. There is so much hurt, pain, heartache, and sorrow in a hospital. I was putting on weight, gaining strength, and generally doing better overall. My legs were getting stronger, I was becoming more audible, and I had more hand–eye coordination. I still was unable to walk, crawl, or shoot a basketball, but I was coming along.

I was always a little sickly, meaning I would get colds easily, and sometimes they would move to my lungs. Then I would have bronchitis, which is not a bunch of fun. Sometimes I would cough and hack up these big, green goobers. You know what a goober is, don't you? Anyway, I needed a lot of care, so Mom had some really nice girls help me. There were several who helped me during the first few years, but Michelle and I became such good buddies. She was my bestest friend. I really liked hanging out with her; we always had a great time together. She would play with me, sing to me, and care for me, just like my mom and dad. Elizabeth was another girl I really liked to be with. She was kind of like my girlfriend. I always kind of had a thing for older women, and of course I did not know younger women! Mom and Dad really needed help because I kept them busy 24/7! These girls were an immeasurable blessing to me. They represented the love of my Divine Daddy to me and to Mom and Dad.

I was so thankful for those people who got to know me and did not let my condition intimidate them. You know what I think happens sometimes? I think people get scared and do not know how to express the love they really wish to show because someone has a disability. They focus on the disability rather than the person. It's really fear—fear of inadequacy, fear of failure, or fear of just not knowing how to connect. Fear paralyzes people in so many ways. At least that is what I have observed from my crib and high chair. The other thing I think people struggle with is guilt. They see a kid like me who may appear to be less than perfect in their eyes (but is still perfect in God's eyes), and they feel guilty. Maybe it's because their children don't have the same challenges. Like fear, guilt can paralyze people. The truth of the matter is that people or kids who have disabilities just want to be treated like everyone else. There were lots of times I wanted to tell people to just treat me like the rest of kids! *Hold me! Talk to me! Play with me! Just be my friend!* That's what all of us VIP kids want. We just want to be treated like kids! Because we are!

The truth of the matter is that people or kids who have disabilities just want to be treated like everyone else.

One of the reasons I needed so much care was that I was still fed through a G-tube, and I threw up a lot. We were not sure why, but I would burp up my food on a regular basis. That meant mega washloads of clothes. It would not be uncommon for me to change almost ten times in a day. You know how hard it is to find matching outfits that many times per day! I didn't mean to, but I know that I brought a lot of extra work to my mom and dad.

There was still a question as to whether my skull plates had prematurely grown together once again. I had bumps on my head, and Mom and Dad were concerned that there was pressure in my head that was causing me to throw up. No one could bear the thought of another surgery, but it had to be considered because Mom and Dad wanted to give me every chance possible to develop. Once again, they sought second and third opinions from Shands Hospital. We even flew up to Boston Children's Hospital to get their opinions on October 5, 1998. It was the first time I had seen leaves change color. My Divine Daddy was pretty creative when He painted all those leaves different colors, not to mention how He has colored the sky with those awesome sunsets.

Once again, I was back in the hospital for yet another skull surgery. This was not an exciting thought for anyone. Mom and Dad joked that I was probably the most prayed-for little boy in Orlando. I think it might have been true. Those prayers kept me alive so my purpose could be fulfilled; at least that is what I have come to believe. I think we all have purpose. Otherwise, why would our Divine Daddy have created us?

Well, this surgery, though emotionally exhausting for Mom and Dad, went about as well as it could. I was out of the hospital in about three days. Mom and Dad hoped this would be the last time I would ever have to be in a hospital. I was at home healing.

I did not know if I was going to be able to run and jump like other kids, but I hoped so. Either way, I knew my Divine Daddy would make something beautiful out of my life because that is His business. You know, He could do just that, just like making a diamond out of a chunk of coal, or a pearl out of an oyster. Who would have thunk it?

JUST SAY "HI!"

"My command is this: Love each other as I have loved you."
—John 15:12, NIV

It can get lonely for a VIP kid (a kid with special needs). Play dates and party invitations are not always freely extended to VIP kids because fear keeps those around them from reaching out. *Everyone* needs love and to feel part of a community. While parents may work hard to bring community to their children, what can the average person do to engage? Start by saying "Hi!"

Instead of looking away, acknowledge a kid (or older person) with a disability. They are kids who happen to have disabilities. But kids first. *All* kids need to be loved and feel a sense of belonging. If we are afraid of what we do not know, then one of the ways to get over our fear is to step out and get to know someone with a disability. There are so many ways to invite a VIP kid into your life, just like you would any other child. Kids are kids. Just be intentional about including VIP kids to events like birthday parties, even if you are initially a little uncomfortable or need to make a few adaptations. As you add to their life, you may soon find that the friendship will be reciprocated in greater ways than you can ever imagine! And as you do, you will also be teaching others about the value of every life.

On the journey together as a family.

CHAPTER FOURTEEN

A PLACE CALLED APATHY

"Apathy is the glove into which evil slips its hand."

—Bodie Thoene,

American Author

It was about this time that Dad was growing a little weary from the constant barrage of sickness and surgeries. He found himself becoming apathetic, with no energy, and kind of without hope. I am told the dictionary defines *apathetic* as "indifferent and unenergetic: not taking any interest in anything, or not bothering to do anything."

Dad was asked to speak at a men's group, and even though Dad was very close with the pastor, he did not even really recognize how emotionally sick he was. It was when he was preparing to speak at a men's group that he came to realize his emotional condition. Then God gave him an analogy that mirrored his emotional state.

Dad had this picture in his mind that he was in a place called Apathy. It was like he was on the road trip of life, weary from a long journey, and he saw a sign that said "Exit in two miles for Apathy, a City without Hope." He knew he needed gas, so he said, "Hey, why not stop here?" As he pulled off the highway, he found that the place called Apathy was in a cold, thick, damp fog. There was no visibility; he couldn't see his hand in front of his face. It was bone-chilling cold, and Dad could not help but feel alone, fearful, powerless, and consumed by a gripping sense of despair.

Apathy had stolen Dad's energy; it was like having water in his high-octane fuel for life. Dad's emotional and even physical engine would not run. Though it made no sense, Dad got gas and picked up a flier and started looking for real estate thinking maybe I should live here. Dad started to like the place he loathed, even though he was lonely, cold, fearful, and gray without color and without hope.

Without an explanation or change in the circumstances, and only by the grace of God, Dad jumped back into the car and got back on the interstate. Somehow he escaped the place called Apathy. As soon as he left the city limits, visibility began to clear. He saw a sign in the distance that said, "Ten miles ahead—A Place Called Hope, a City on a Hill, a Land of Limitless Possibilities." The dictionary states that *hope* is "the feeling that what is wanted can be had or that events will turn out for the best." He took a chance and put on his blinker for a place called Hope. Immediately he saw the contrast between a place called Apathy and a place called Hope. A place called Hope was fresh, liberating, bright, and full of energy and seemingly unlimited 360-degree visibility. The air was cool and crisp, and it gave Dad energy. The colors were vibrant, and there was a sense of anticipation in the air. Anything seemed possible in this place called Hope, while nothing seemed to be possible in the place called Apathy. Dad's weariness left, and he was rejuvenated and renewed for the journey ahead.

Though the circumstances did not change, by the grace of God, Dad could grasp the truth in the Scripture that states, "And we know that in all things God works for the good of those who love him, who have been called according to his purpose" (Rom. 8:28, NIV). Even though many challenges were ahead, with God all things are possible. Dad realized his responsibility is to do the possible; God must do the impossible. Dad was invigorated in the place called Hope. He had the high-octane fuel of Hope for the rest of his road trip in life.

Like Father, like son.

CHAPTER FIFTEEN

THIRD TIME IS A CHARM. NOT!

"You will suffer for a while, but God will make you complete, steady, strong, and firm."

—1 Peter 5:10, CEV

In the spring of 2000, Mom and Dad sought counsel once again about my head. I was still throwing up my food, and bumps began to protrude again. They called all over the country, and they decided to fly me to Dallas to see some cranial facial specialists. Mom and Dad were impressed with the doctors' counsel, and they decided to pursue a third surgery on my head. You know that saying, "Third time is a charm"? Well, that is a stupid saying. Who came up with that, anyway? Why not say that the first time is a charm?

After my mom and dad prayed through the decision, they decided to proceed with the surgery, which was going to take place in Dallas, not at the close-to-home, comfortable surroundings of our kids' hospital. We had tried to communicate regularly with our friends and family. Then Mom and Dad helped me write this letter.

From Nathaniel...

Dear Family and Friends,

I know it's a "big surprise" to hear from us twice in one year, but this year we have lots to tell! I've been keeping my mom and dad pretty busy since my surgery this past September. I really needed the skull expansion surgery. There didn't seem to be a whole lot of room left in my skull for my brain to grow. After the surgery, I felt a lot better; I stopped vomiting and started to really begin to do a lot of new things developmentally. I was even able to take food from a spoon! (Chocolate pudding is pretty yummy!) But then in November, I started vomiting again and even got pneumonia. Then in January, I really had a bad pneumonia and even had to go to the hospital for a few days and come home on oxygen. Since then, I don't sleep very good. Mom and I know the 3:00 a.m. lineup on TV pretty well. I'm still vomiting, too. So I guess I have been pretty fussy lately; maybe that's why. Because I'm his special boy, my dad did a lot of research on the internet and talked to quite a few doctors out of state trying to find a specialized doctor to try to help me. Dad, Mom, and I took a plane ride to Dallas, where we met with a team of doctors called a cranial-facial team. They do a lot of surgeries on kids' heads at this hospital, so I think they are pretty good at it. Dad says, "This is their itch, or was that their niche!"

These doctors believe another surgery is necessary and hope it will help me have more room for my brain to grow so that I will continue to be able to develop.

So, next week on July 5, my whole family is going to take me back to Dallas for surgery. I'm really glad that my sisters can be with me. I am scheduled for surgery on Friday, July 7, at about noon, Dallas time.

This is going to be a pretty big surgery—maybe four to five hours. The doctors are going to do some big reconstruction of my skull, a lot of work at the front of my head. I know it's going to be tough, but we are all trusting in God to take care of me.

God has been teaching Mom and Dad a lot through this journey. My dad says he recently read this in James 1: 2–4: "Consider it pure joy, my brothers and sisters, whenever you face trials of many kinds, because you know that the testing of your faith produces perseverance. Let perseverance finish its work so that you may be mature and complete, not lacking anything." He said he isn't grown up enough to "consider it pure joy," but he has found comfort in "letting perseverance finish its work." Though life's journey can be long and hard, we can learn to expect "to be mature and complete, not lacking anything," through those hardships and trials. I think that Dad is growing up in more ways than he knows!

I love my dad and mom and sure depend on them a whole lot to take care of me. Who else would be willing to hang out with me all night? I just couldn't survive without their care. But you know what? My dad and mom need me just as much as I need them. We are interdependent. That is God's plan. God's ways are higher than our ways. His ways and desires are to develop His character in Dad and Mom, and He uses me to help do that! We need each other for God's perfect result. And all of us are for sure dependent on God. What would we do without Him?

That's good preaching stuff! I bet that Dad will probably steal these great sermon notes from me one day!

Thanks for taking the time to listen. I feel better knowing you will be praying for me because I know that God really hears your prayers.

But best of all, I know that God holds me in the palm of His hand.

God Bless You!
Love,
Nathaniel

We flew to Dallas for the surgery. I kind of like flying. My sisters came with me, along with Mom, Dad and Michelle.

Michelle was a great support because she knew my sisters and me so well. I was so grateful that my family always stayed with me when I had to do these tough things. Somebody was always at my side. *Always!* Of course I know that God was really with me all the time, even when I was in the operating room. As we were on the way to the hospital from the hotel, we were all thinking about the big surgery I was going to be facing. Dad turned on the radio. There was a song he had heard once before that was like a prayer from his heart. That morning, it was a reminder that God was listening to our anxious hearts. It was a song written by Christian recording artist Mark Schultz who had walked the journey of cancer with one of the teens in his youth group, and it went like this:

"He's My Son"

I'm down on my knees again tonight,
I'm hoping this prayer will turn out right.
See, there's a boy that needs Your help.
I've done all that I can do myself
His mother is tired,
I'm sure You can understand.
Each night as he sleeps
She goes in and holds his hand,
And she tries not to cry
As the tears fill her eyes.
Can You hear me?
Am I getting through tonight?
Can You see him?

Can You make him feel all right?
If You can hear me
Let me take his place somehow.
You see, he's not just anyone,
He's my son.
Sometimes late at night
I watch him sleep,
I dream of the boy he'd like to be.
I try to be strong and see him through,
But God who he needs right now is You.
Let him grow old,
Live life without this fear.
What would I be
Living without him here?
He's so tired and he's so scared
Let me know that You're there.
See, he's not just anyone.
Can You hear me?
Can You see him?
He's my son.[1]

"Leave all your worries with him, because He cares for you."
—1 Peter 5:7, GNT

---

4. Mark Schultz, "He's My Son." Lyrics by Don Robey, George Hollis. Copyright © Universal Music Publishing Group.

CHAPTER SIXTEEN

LIFE HAS PURPOSE

"'For I know the plans I have for you,'
declares the LORD, 'plans to prosper you
and not to harm you, plans to give you
hope and a future.'"
—Jeremiah 29:11, NIV

Actually, Dallas was much more difficult than we anticipated. Everything turned out pretty good except that I contracted pneumonia once again.

But my Divine Daddy was not ready for me to leave Earth yet. I spent about twelve days in the Pediatric Intensive Care Unit, and finally I was moved to a regular room. As we were moving into my new room, something kind of strange happened. As my mom and dad were dragging all our stuff into the room, my new nurse was standing over my bed, weeping. She kept saying, "There is something about this boy. There is something about this boy." She said she had never done or felt anything like this before. Mom and Dad were a little perplexed by the circumstances but wanted to get to know my new caregiver.

After we settled into the room, Mom and Dad began to chat with the nurse. As they talked, Mom and Dad found out that my nurse knew my Divine Daddy, too. After some discussion, the nurse asked if she could pray for us. They said, "Sure, we need all the prayers we can get." The nurse prayed that my purpose would be fulfilled. What in the world did that mean? We expected a prayer for my healing and strength, not that my purpose would be fulfilled. Mom and Dad commented about that unusual prayer, and they even journaled about it.

The nurse prayed that my purpose would be fulfilled.

When we arrived home, a friend of my mom's named Doneta, who was a nurse living in Minneapolis, flew down to help care for me. I was on an IV, receiving three injections per day; plus, I was being treated with the nebulizer every couple of hours. You know, the nebulizer was that vapor mist stuff you breathe and it makes you breathe easier. Dad said that Doneta was like an angel. She came when we needed care the most. She was an immeasurable blessing to my family and me. She is a little silly, though, and made us smile a lot. Dad would joke with her and say, "Just remember, our house is not your house." But she is part of our family, just like Michelle. It is amazing how many girlfriends I have for being only three years old; I must be some kind of handsome hunk. Like a chick magnet!

REST FOR THE CAREGIVERS

"Take my yoke upon you and learn from me, for I am gentle and humble in heart, and you will find rest for your souls."
— Matthew 11:29, NIV

One of the greatest needs that families who have kids with disabilities have is to get a break. Many moms and dads are in caregiver mode 24/7. The weight and stress of finding proper doctors, teachers, financial resources, and other needs for a VIP child's care can be overwhelming for caregivers. Those responsibilities, as well as the never-ending demands for the daily care of their child, are squeezed into days already filled with the usual routine of caring for a household, siblings, and self. Typically, self is the last priority on the list. When operating in survival mode, it is often a challenge to even recognize and justify the luxury of rest. It is important for caregivers to find ways to get rest and care for themselves so they don't burn out and find themselves unable to provide care for their loved one.

The reality is that it can be tough for families to find qualified caregivers to care for their kids. Most caregivers are not able to call the girl down the street to baby-sit. Many times, well-meaning family members do not recognize the need or are not available to help.

Nathaniel's Hope has created a way for caring individuals to GIVE A BREAK or for VIP families to GET A BREAK through the Buddy Break program, a FREE kids respite program where kids with special needs (VIP kids) make new friends and enjoy all types of fun activities, while caregivers get a much-needed break. This program is provided in partnership with local churches around the country.

For more information about how you can join the network as a provider or get respite, visit www.NathanielsHope.org.

Nathaniel's little life had a lasting impact on his big sisters.

CHAPTER SEVENTEEN

A SEASON OF BLESSING

"Surely you have granted him unending blessings and made him glad with the joy of your presence."

—Psalm 21:6, NIV

I thought it was time to check in with everyone. I just want to share this special time my family and me are having because of the blessings of better health and less trouble.

Dear Family and Friends,

Hi, everybody! It's me, Nathaniel! Sorry it's taken so long to write to you again, but I've still been keeping my mom and dad pretty busy. I've heard them say that no news is good news, whatever that means.

Well, I survived my big trip to Dallas. It was not my idea of a vacation. In case you haven't heard, let me tell you about it. The surgery took about five hours and went well, other than my coming out with a pretty big headache! The doctors said I needed a little more room in my skull, and they were also able to take the big bumps out. Mom said I looked pretty swollen, like ET, but now my head is rounder, and I look more handsome...like my dad! That was the good part.

The not-so-good part was that I had to go back on the ventilator (breathing machine) twice after surgery because I caught a bacterial pneumonia. Things didn't look so good for a while because 80 percent of my left lung shut down overnight, and the antibiotics weren't helping me. I heard the doctor tell my mom and dad that this was a "life-threatening situation." I'm so thankful that God stayed with me and held me tightly in the palm of His hand...especially through those really tough days. I think my mom and dad learned a big lesson in trusting and surrendering to God. (Dad is a slow learner; he thought he had already been there, done that, a few times before.) After I was in the hospital for twelve days, Mom and Dad were determined to take me home, even though I was on oxygen. Dorothy was right when she said, "There's no place like home." At home I could finally rest! (The words "hospital" and "rest" just don't go together...everybody was sticking and picking on me all day and night!) It took me a while to get over my addiction to all the narcotics. No joke! I had to go on methadone! How many three-year-olds go through that experience?

I am doing so much better now! I have put on four whole pounds since surgery! That's more than 20 percent of my body weight. I weigh twenty-two pounds now, the most I have ever weighed my whole life! My sisters affectionately call me "Pork Chop" since I have some fat on me (I even have love handles, like my dad). I am getting stronger and have been able to do some new things. I'm so excited!

I'm also not throwing up like I used to, either. I guess my head was really affecting a lot of stuff.

It's hard to believe that seven weeks have already passed. I'll bet you're wondering how Mom and Dad are holding up after all this.

My dad says, "It is only a faded memory now. The nights in ICU, my Nathaniel on the ventilator fighting to survive. The twelve days in Dallas seem to be a blur, now only a distant memory. What I do know and remember is this: life can be hard—grueling at times—but God is faithful. It is not until the iron is thrust into the glow of white-hot flames that it can be shaped, bent, and formed. After the fire, the iron is not the same in form or strength. It is now tempered by the heat, stronger than before. The form has been altered, skillfully forming every delicate and intricate detail. Even before the iron went into the furnace, the Master Creator saw and knew the out-come He desired.

It is in the fire of trial that our faith has once again been forged. It has taken new dimension and strength. There in the heat of the fire, we must decide if we will trust God, regardless of the outcome. It is there that our faith takes new shape as we entrust our circumstances to the hands of the Master, knowing the outcome is in His hands, not ours.

Romans 5:1–5 (CEV) says it this way:

"By faith we have been made acceptable to God. And now, because of our Lord Jesus Christ, we live at peace with God. Christ has also introduced us to God's undeserved kindness on which we take our stand. So we are happy, as we look forward to sharing in the glory of God. But that's not all! We gladly suffer, because we know that suffering helps us to endure. And endurance builds character, which gives us a hope that will never disappoint us. All of this happens because God has given us the Holy Spirit, who fills our hearts with his love."

Dad says we all have our trials, but God's purpose and desire are to work through them in our lives so He might be glorified. His grace is sufficient in our weakness.

This is all pretty deep for me, but maybe you can relate with Dad.

Mom is starting to get some better sleep, thanks to me. I'm starting to sleep between four to six hours without waking up! I'm still trying to decide if I am going to do this all the time (hee-hee).

So what's the future plan? The doctors say there is a small chance that they might need to repeat this surgery in a year (easy for them to say)!

Thank you for all the calls, cards, emails, meals, presents, love, encouragement, and most important, the prayers...we could've never made it without them. They literally sustained us for weeks.

That's all for now.

I love and appreciate you more than you'll ever know!

Nathaniel

I am now about three and a half years old, and things have finally settled down; at least nothing major is going on. Mom still sleeps on the floor next to me in the living room because I do not sleep very well. I really never have; I really hated that because I knew that Mom was wearing out. She would get up with me at all times during the night to care for me. Sometimes we would watch *The Dating Game* together to pass the time. My Divine Daddy really knew what He was doing when He gave me Mommy. I don't think there was anyone on Earth who could love and care for me like her. She always puts me first; she is always there for me.

My sisters, Brianna and Ashley, are such fun for me to be with, too. They always let me know how much they love me, and they spend lots of time playing with me and helping me do fun things. I'm so lucky because my Divine Daddy gave me two special big sisters to love and be loved by.

A Sister's Perspective...

Being a sibling to someone with special needs definitely wasn't easy. Looking back on my childhood, there are a lot of things I missed out on. My parents did their best to make life for us as normal as possible. But let's face it—having a little brother with a million different special needs isn't exactly normal. Every once in a while, I will still get questions about my childhood. People are shocked to find out that I didn't have many friends outside of my family members or that I didn't get to do some of the normal childhood activities. And although playdates are really good and important things for kids growing up, they aren't nearly as important as making sure your youngest sibling has what he needs to survive day to day. So we mostly stuck to hanging out with each other and with our cousins.

I never really minded it so much, though. Maybe I just didn't know what I was missing out on. Or maybe I was able to see the beauty in the challenge of having a little brother with special needs. We cherished the days that we would hold him, dancing around the living room floor, playing with his

Cookie Monster toy that always made him smile, or pulling him around the house on a blanket since he couldn't run around with us himself. All the long days in the hospital and the times we had to help take care of him brought us together in the most special way. We became a solid family unit. That means when there was something that Nathaniel couldn't do, then none of us wanted to do it. We always wanted our little brother to be able to experience life with us.

Looking back, I am so thankful that I got to have Nathaniel for a little brother, even though it was just for a few short years. There will always be the questions of "What if he didn't have special needs?" or "What if he were still with us today?" But it is undeniable the purpose that God had in his short little life. Not only in the way that he changed me and changed my family, but also in the many lives that have been impacted by Nathaniel's Hope.

Ashley,
Nathaniel's sister

REMEMBER SIBLINGS

Being the sibling of a child with special needs isn't easy. It's important to recognize that siblings have unique needs also, and their voices deserve to be heard. Often, siblings feel unnoticed or neglected as attention is focused on their brother or sister with special needs, but they need to feel that their needs are important, too. They need support of their own—someone to talk with, someone to feel close to, and someone who sees the need behind whatever behavior they exhibit.

It is hard for siblings to form secure attachments to the primary caregiving parent. So much time and energy are required for the child with special needs that other children in the family often feel invisible. If you are close to a special-needs family, be intentional to notice the siblings. You can be the comfort they crave and the listening ear for their hurts and joys.

While they may face a difficult journey, this journey can also be the catalyst for their own unique life purpose. This has been true for our daughter, Brianna. She is now passionate about helping kids (siblings) work through their trauma.

Nathaniel's contagious smile.

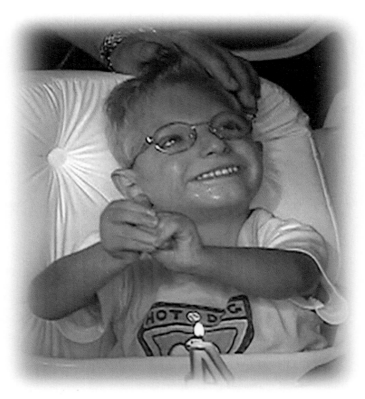

Celebrating Nathaniel's 4th Birthday!

CHAPTER EIGHTEEN

A SEASON OF HOPE

"May the God of hope fill you with all joy and peace as you trust in him, so that you may overflow with hope..."
—Romans 15:13, NIV

It is now nearing Christmas. I really, really like Christmas. The house has familiar smells, and I get new toys. The whole family goes out to get a Christmas tree together. This is the great news: I am not in the hospital. But Mom and Dad remember how sad it was being at the hospital on Christmas Day. So they decided to bring the "real hope" of Christmas to the hospital. On Christmas Day, Mom and Dad started a group now called "Caroling for Kids" at my kids' hospital to bring encouragement and hope to those stuck there away from home on Christmas. We want to bring hope to other kids like me because hope changes everything! It seems like everyone could use more hope. I think that is why my Divine Daddy sent us His son, Jesus.

We did our best to try to keep in touch with our friends and family during this season. We sent this special Christmas letter in December 2000.

From Nathaniel's High Chair...

Dear Family and Friends,

It's beginning to look a lot like Christmas around here, and that makes me feel thankful! I just want to take the time to say "Thank you" to God for taking care of me and to you for all your faithful prayers. I know they continue to help me.

This has been a kinda rough season for me, with lots of coughs and colds going around our family (our family likes to share everything)! I had bronchitis a few times and even a small pneumonia. Please pray that my lungs will continue to get stronger.

When I'm feeling good, I've been working really hard with my mom, dad, sisters, and therapists. They are really excited about some of the new things I'm doing. It may take me a little longer to learn stuff, but it feels really good when I hit new milestones. Keep praying! Dad's favorite is when I play for him (or make noise) on the piano. Who is Mozart ,anyway?

I love Christmas! All the lights and the fun things to smell and taste...and what about those presents! I can't wait to see what's in those packages Mom has been hiding! I love to get gifts, but the best gift of Christmas is Jesus! He's the one who gives me life every day...in every way!

I hope you experience the gift of Jesus in every way this Christmas and the whole year through!

Merry Christmas!!!
Love,
Nathaniel Kuck & family

After Christmas, things were pretty much "normal" at the Kuck house. We did something really cool in May after my sisters got out of school: we went away and celebrated Grandpa and Grandma's fiftieth wedding anniversary. All my Kuck cousins and my aunts and uncles were there for almost a week—nineteen of us in all, including Michelle. That was really fun. Grandpa and Grandma told us the story of their lives, starting from the beginning. Mom and Dad recorded almost six hours on video. We finally got to do something pretty "normal."

It was great. It was the best time I had ever had with my

cousins.

We really never had had a summer vacation because of my sickness and surgeries, but this year, we spent almost a week in the Bahamas. This made Dad happy, as he loved boating and had not been able to cruise for a long time. I did not put on scuba tanks or anything, but isn't one of the greatest things in the world being with your family? Those people who love you unconditionally, no matter what. You see, I know my mom and dad will always love me; they would never abandon me to do just what they please. Don't you think we should all love more people unconditionally and not base love on performance? I heard Jesus said that it is better to give than receive, and giving is a big part of unconditional love.

Before I knew it, summer had come and gone, and fall was almost here. Actually, I think I had the best summer of my life; there is nothing like making memories with the family.

We had decided to get a special picture for Grandpa and Grandma for their actual anniversary, which was on October 21. So all eighteen of us got together to take this picture. Some people might say it is hard to get a good picture of me because I won't sit still, but this photographer had a digital camera, so it was easy to cut and paste (I think that is something you do in kindergarten art class). We got some great pictures, including one of just the five members of our family. This would always be a special place in time to remember.

BE INTENTIONAL ABOUT REACHING OUT TO THE ENTIRE FAMILY

The daily life of a VIP family can be all-consuming. In many cases, this lifestyle never goes away—it lasts for a lifetime. Caring for a loved one 24/7 can be exhausting, isolating, and overwhelming. Making an intentional effort to reach out to and care for the family/caregiver is something practical that family and friends can do to be a support. The simple act of meeting a friend for coffee is a pleasure that might not be possible. Why not offer to bring coffee over and share an hour of friendship? Small gestures like this can pull a family member out of isolation and bring hope to a weary soul. Be practical! Next time you go to the grocery store, why not ask if you can pick up some groceries? Offer to take a sibling to a school or church event. Prepare a meal, or better yet, share a meal together. Send a prayerful text, or leave an encouraging message to remind them that they are not forgotten. Remember, many families are on this journey for a lifetime. Most families will live in survival mode and find it difficult to reach out and ask for help. Or if they do say "Help!" few may hear them. It's important to remember that these families are not running a sprint but rather a marathon. Your consistent efforts to intentionally reach out and care for a family can be critical for their survival.

"Truly I tell you, whatever you did for one of the least of these brothers and sisters of mine, you did for me."
—Matthew 25:40, NIV

Our Family photo – October 1997
An irreplaceable moment in time.

CHAPTER NINETEEN

CHANGE OF ADDRESS

"But our citizenship is in heaven. And we eagerly await a Savior from there, the Lord Jesus Christ, who, by the power that enables him to bring everything under his control, will transform our lowly bodies so that they will be like his glorious body."

—Philippians 3:20–21, NIV

October had now passed, and we were into November. There was a lot of activity in the house because Dad was going to speak at a couple of churches in Illinois, so he was going to be gone for a few days. Dad did not travel much since I was born, so he usually was home every night. Before he left, Mom and Dad stopped by a leadership retreat that their church was having so everyone could pray for our family. At that time, Mom and Dad really couldn't do too much to lead any areas of ministry, but Pastor Chris and their church family were so loving and caring and believed that talking to Divine Daddy in prayer made a difference. They always did their best to love on our family.

Mom worked with the ladies of the church and often heard complaints being shared about the nursery not doing enough for the kids. At this retreat, Mom made a comment that she was frustrated because while folks were complaining about the services of the nursery, kids with special needs had nothing. She thought someone should put something together for this community of special-needs kids and parents. The team kindly listened and prayed for Mom and Dad.

Mom helped Dad get packed, and on Saturday afternoon, November 9, Dad left. I remember we all took him to the airport. Dad walked around the van, and he opened the door to give me a kiss on the head while I was in my car seat. I liked it when Dad kissed me on the head, and I especially liked this kiss.

Mom talked to Dad that night, and then on Sunday. Mom told Dad I had gotten a little sick, but it seemed manageable. On Monday, Mom told Dad that my condition had worsened. I was having a little trouble breathing, and I was generally fussy. I really would not eat anything, and I just could not sleep. I was sick, but I had been much sicker than this before. Mom went ahead and made a doctor's appointment with Dr. D for Tuesday morning, November 13, at 9:30 a.m. Mom talked to Dad on Monday night and said that I was very fussy and would not sleep. Believe me, I *wanted* to sleep; I just couldn't. You know what I mean. Mom talked to Dad later that same night, about 11:00 p.m. Central Time, and she said she was concerned that my condition was worsening. She thought that if I would sleep, I would be okay.

During the night, Mom tried to help me feel better. She did all the things that normally worked to make me feel better. But that night, nothing worked. There was something different. I just kept feeling worse. Why was Daddy God not helping? I could tell that Mom was worried. She talked to Daddy and wondered if she should take me to the hospital, but I had an appointment with Dr. D the next morning. My sisters were sleeping, so she was all alone and didn't know what to do. I felt really yucky. Mom tried everything to comfort me. Nothing helped. Even the oxygen didn't make me feel better. It was a long night. I don't think I finally fell asleep until early morning in my mom's arms. I took a breath, and I remember her looking at me a little funny. But before I could respond back to her, my breath was taken away... *as I saw Him*! My Divine Daddy! He was coming to me with His arms wide open and was calling me to come to Him. I didn't want to leave my mom, but before I could stop myself, I saw myself running to Him. Wait! *I was running!!! I was sprinting!* In fact, I wanted to dance! I was not feeling yucky anymore. *I was free!*

But then I turned to look back to see if my mom could see

me. It was like a movie in the distance. I saw my mom crying as she was trying to help me. She was trying to breathe life into me, but she couldn't. She was helpless. I watched my sister, Brianna, look at me just lying there, and then I was carried into an ambulance. Mom ran to the ambulance to go with me and left my sisters to wait for the neighbor and Grandpa to come. The paramedics tried to tried to get my heart to work. I wanted to scream out, *"Look at me!* I am with my Divine Daddy!"

CHAPTER TWENTY

IN A MOMENT, EVERYTHING CHANGED

(Letters from the Family)

A Sister's Perspective...

Most of the time, Nathaniel's homecoming feels surreal to me, but sometimes it feels like yesterday. It wasn't. November 13, 2001—that difficult day began at 6:15 a.m.

"Brianna, get the phone, and get a wet rag! Nathaniel stopped breathing!" my mom yelled frantically.

It was a whirlwind.

"Ma'am, we have to leave now!" is the next thing I remember. It was the paramedic's booming voice as he followed my mom into her bedroom. She had quickly gone to change clothes, but there wasn't time.

My brother had already been rushed into the ambulance.

Then, silence.

Just like that, they were all gone. A sudden stillness overcame our house.

My nine-year-old self was now alone to wake up my seven-year-old sister, Ashley.

Nathaniel had been in the hospital many times before. This was just one of those times, right? We continued our morning per usual and carpooled to choir at 7:15 a.m. Our uncle picked us up from school at around 9:30 a.m. He managed small talk as he took us to the hospital.

We walked in, and there were people there, lots of family friends scattered outside and in the lobby. My sister and I were ushered into a waiting room, soon to be greeted by our parents. It was then that my life would change forever.

"Nathaniel went to heaven this morning," they said, faces downcast and distorted with emotion.

He was gone. Without warning.

"No, no, no, no, no! This can't be happening!" I screamed in my head. It was too much for me to understand or handle as a fourth-grader.

The four of us left the waiting room and were led down a hallway into a dark, seemingly empty room. Empty because it had no life. They pulled a sheet back, and there he was—cold, pale, lifeless. The remains of my baby brother, our precious little man around whom our lives had revolved for the past four and a half years.

It was there that we said our good-byes. It was then that our family of five became a family of four.

Brianna,
Nathaniel's sister

——————————— ... ———————————

A Mother's Perspective...

The days that followed are too painful to adequately put into words. In a moment, everything changed forever. It seemed like a really bad dream, not our reality. It felt like after running at a pace of one hundred miles per hour, we hit a wall. It was a shock. And it really hurt.

For four and a half years, we had fought for our son's life. We left no stone unturned. We sacrificed in every way to care for him. Our entire family was devoted to Nathaniel's needs. Every decision we made was made based on what was best for him. Then in an instant—just like that—life changed. And there was nothing I could do to fix it.

The silence in the house was eerie. The echoes of machines and gurgly noises were now drowned out by an empty silence. Life lost its color. We were now seeing life as a black-and-white film. Would life ever be normal again?

It was difficult for us to help each other as family. We all processed this loss differently. While it brought comfort for me to be with people, Tim dealt with his pain by withdrawing from everyone. Our girls seemed to be processing, but in reality, tried to hide their pain in an effort to keep from burdening us.

We knew that God had carried us on this journey, and we had witnessed miracle after miracle. So why did it end like this? After wrestling with my theology, I remembered what King David said after losing his son: "Someday, I will join him in death, but he can't return to me" (2 Sam. 12:23).

We began to realize that this was not the "real life," that there was an eternity. We would spend eternity not just with Jesus, but with Nathaniel. Our future with Nathaniel was actually going to be greater than our past with him. Bart Millard of Mercy Me expressed it so well in his song, "I Can Only Imagine."

We began to see life a little differently, and "Why God?" turned into "What for, God?"

Marie,
Nathaniel's mom

—————————— ... ——————————

A Christmas Letter from Dad...

December 25, 2001

Dear Family,

Today we celebrate Christmas, the birth of Jesus, our Savior. This usual time of joy has been clouded by sadness and sorrow due to the absence of Nathaniel.

Though I have looked for an escape from this place of heartache, I have not found a place to hide but have come to understand all too well that grieving is a journey. There are no quick fixes, inspiring words, or Scriptures that can quickly heal this wound. Though the road on the journey is difficult, God has been gracious nonetheless.

Consistent with the character of God in Scripture, God's ways are higher than our ways, and He has chosen to use this season of sorrow as a schoolroom for the Schoolmaster to teach. We are now students in a class we did not elect to take but are required to finish. So we will now go about our daily lives, attempting to learn the lesson, which we would rather not know, but knowing somehow that God will show us.

I realize that things are, and have been, a little strained and awkward for you as well, for you are our companions on this journey. We feel a very tangible sense of how much you want to help to heal our pain. Whatever words could be said, or acts of love and kindness shown, they can at best be a soothing ointment bringing temporary relief. The healing will take God and time. We may not seem to be appreciative or grateful for your outstretched hands and hearts, but we are so thankful for your support. You have made this stretch of road in our journey in life bearable. Your unconditional love and support have been a tangible substance from Nathaniel's birth until now. You are doing all that can be done, and we are blessed to have you as family.

I wish things were different and our grieving circumstances did not ripple into your lives, but I cannot wish it into being. It is what it is. Scripture tells us that we are to mourn with those who mourn, and those who mourn shall be comforted. I am grateful for the Comforter and the strength we have to hold tightly to the taut rope of Hope, which is our Father in Heaven. Nathaniel has graduated and now has a greater understanding of "The Hope" than we can even begin to imagine. Until then, we can exercise our hearts and minds and imagine what it would be like to be there with Nathaniel and others who have gone before us, worshipping the Creator of the Universe.

Do you remember the story I told you about the nurse who prayed that His purpose would be fulfilled? This book is part of that purpose. I heard a quote by Soren Kierkegaard that says, "We live life forward, but we understand life backward." Only now can we begin to understand that is part of God's purpose and plan.

I love you, and I thank God for you. He has shown us His love through you.

Tim,

Nathaniel's dad

——————————— ... ———————————

A Dad's Perspective...

In January, I was still emotionally struggling. I would have a good day now and then, but it did not seem like I was making progress. To tell the truth, I did not care if I lived or died. Now, that makes no rational sense, but it was reflective of my emotional state. Even though spiritually I knew I would see my son again and I had everything to live for, I was emotionally sick. A rational approach was not going to cure my emotional sickness. It is like taking an antibiotic for a virus; it does not cure the sickness.

As I was going through this part of the grieving process, I had a picture in my mind. It was like I was crossing a raging river of grief. It was really wide-so wide I could not see the other side. Stretching across the river was a rope that was taut. I was dangling with my head just above the water, holding on to the rope. Slowly, I placed one hand in front of the other, making my way across this river. There was a torrential, violent current, and just when I thought I was beginning to make progress, I wass hit with a fast-moving, rogue wave of grief. It would knock me under the current, but I was still hanging on to the rope that was hope in Christ. Even though I could not see the other side, I knew it was there because the rope was taut. I needed to persevere, holding on to that rope with one hand and then healing had begun. The distance between the rogue waves of grief had become greater, but I still had a long way to go. In March, our family took a trip to Colorado during our daughters' spring break. It was just what my family needed to accelerate our healing. Everyone had an awesome time. We laughed and cried, but healing had accelerated.

"Us" Kucks are kind of like the Griswolds when we travel, so there are always special moments and hilarious stories. Proverbs states that "a merry heart doeth good like medicine." My family needed laughter, which was medicine, and it helped bring healing.

Tim,

Nathaniel's dad

WAYS TO HELP A GRIEVING FAMILY

Grief is painful. Abrupt loss brings lifelong impact to the entire family. At times it's ugly. It is not natural for parents to outlive their children or for siblings to have to say good-bye to their brother or sister. Grandparents not only grieve the loss of a grandchild; they also watch helplessly as their own child suffers the unbearable pain of their loss. What can you do to help? Here are some simple ways to show your support to a grieving family and to help them with the healing process.

1. The most valuable support you can give is to just be there. Be there to listen. Be there to cry with them. Be there to hold them. It's tempting to give advice, but don't. Just be present.

2. Acknowledge their loss with a simple caring statement like, "I'm so sorry for your loss." Don't presume to know the will of God or the depth of the emotions they are facing. You don't have to have answers or fix it.

3. Everyone processes grief differently. Often, family members are not able to help one another. If you think someone is having trouble coping alone, gently recommend a professional who might be able to help. Remember that siblings might need help to process and unpack their feelings about the loss.

4. Be proactive and specific about how you want to help in practical ways. Offer to prepare a meal, help with cleaning, or run an errand for them. Though you mean well, do not

say, "Call me if you need me." Just call them back. They will not call you; they are in survival mode and cannot think clearly.

5.   Reach out at those times when the family will most miss their loved ones. Holidays, birthdays, and anniversaries will be difficult for years to come. A card or phone call to let them know their loved one is not forgotten will be appreciated. Don't be afraid to talk about their loved one, to say his or her name, or share a favorite memory.

6.   Though grief makes us desperate to make changes that will help us escape the pain, encourage the family not to make any major decisions but to take time and rest.

7.   Encourage families with the hope from an eternal perspective.

CONCLUSION

RESERVATION FOR RELOCATION

"And God will wipe away every tear from their eyes; there shall be no more death, nor sorrow, nor crying. There shall be no more pain, for the former things have passed away."

—Revelation 21:4, NKJV

On November 13, 2001, at the young age of only four and a half years old, Nathaniel Timothy Kuck, "A Treasured Gift from God," relocated to 777 Heavenly Lane. He proved himself to be "a miracle boy," beating the odds time and time again by overcoming many physical obstacles and challenges. His purpose has now been fulfilled, and he has now been returned home to His Creator. At his new home, he is no longer physically restricted and no longer bound by surgeries, feeding tubes, or braces. He is now free to run on the streets of gold.

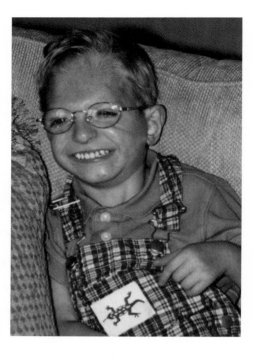

Nathaniel taught us that to each life there is value and purpose. What may appear to be imperfect in the eyes of man really is perfect in the sight of God. He taught us about the meaning of "unconditional love" and perseverance and was a great showcase of God's faithfulness. His captivating smile and the simple joy he brought to all who entered his world was God's special gift and will be greatly missed. His memory will always be cherished, and his little handprints and the lessons he taught us will always be imprinted on our hearts forever.

From Nathaniel...

Hey you guys, guess what! I am now in my heavenly home. It is better than I thought it would be! It truly is paradise!

I just wanted you to know this place is totally awesome! Everybody is full of joy up here! Mom and Dad never told me how cool this place really is. I know they want me back, but my place is here now. I am totally healed and free! No kidding! I have a brand-new body, and now I can run up and down those streets of gold! And the food is out of this world!

You ought to see the real estate up here, and my new digs. Wow! You gotta come check this out. I'll be waiting for you! It is not just for kids—there are lots of grown-ups here, too. Don't forget, the only way you can come is by making a reservation. That cliché "Jesus loves you" is more than a cliché. His love is more real than you can begin to imagine. Remember, it is up to you to receive His love. All for now!

Love,
Nathaniel Timothy Kuck

P.S. Don't wait too long! You might miss your chance!

HAVE YOU MADE YOUR RESERVATION?

To make your reservation at 777 Heavenly Lane, join Nathaniel in this prayer:

Dear Lord Jesus, I know I have done wrong (sinned). I believe that Jesus Christ died on the cross for my sins. Please forgive me of all my sins, and come into my heart and life as my Savior and Lord. Help me to live for You every day. I do not want to just know about You, Jesus—I want to know You as a friend who is closer than a brother. Thank You for forgiving me and for reserving for me an "eternal home" in Nathaniel's neighborhood. In Jesus's name, amen.

THE HOPE AND THE PROMISE

"For the wages of sin is death, but the gift of God is eternal life in Christ Jesus our Lord."
—Romans 6:23, NIV

"If you declare with your mouth, 'Jesus is Lord,' and believe in your heart that God raised him from the dead, you will be saved."
—Romans 10:9, NIV

Final Thoughts...

Nathaniel continues to impact thousands of lives through the outreach of Nathaniel's Hope.

NATHANIEL'S PURPOSE TAKES WINGS

"Therefore, since we are surrounded by such a great cloud of witnesses, let us throw off everything that hinders and the sin that so easily entangles. And let us run with perseverance the race marked out for us."
—Hebrews 12:1, NIV

Soon after Nathaniel moved to heaven to live with his Divine Daddy, we realized that this was not the end, but the beginning. God wanted us to steward our journey with Nathaniel to help and serve others.

When we were fighting hand-to-hand combat for our son's life, I had shared with my coworkers at Regal Boats about the difficult journey our family faced. I shared daily struggles and frustrations, and I told them I did not know how some people make it because it is such a hard journey.

I shared with them five elements that were making a huge difference for our family. I told them about The Five Fs. We were blessed by having these Five Fs at a time when we were barely making it. These Five Fs helped see us through the most difficult of times.

THE 5 Fs

- **Faith** — which is grounded on biblical principles of truth and the knowledge that God works all things together for the good for those who love Him. God will see us through, hold our hands through the immeasurable pain and trauma, and take us to the other side.

- **Family**—Loving, encouraging, and supportive during the exhaustive times in the hospital and beyond.

- **Friends**—Who would walk alongside us consistently to keep us from falling while traversing the treacherous terrain on our journey in life.

- **Finances**—We were not going to lose our car or house while expending considerable finances on caring for our son.

- **Flexibility**—I could miss work and not get fired. I was a member of a family business that extended the grace and flexibility needed because of having a child who spent 150 days in the hospital.

These Five Fs were like legs on a stool or pillars on a building. We wondered, what do people do who have only two or three Fs? How do they make it to the other side and not lose their job, marriage, or sobriety in life—or lose all hope?

Hope Sustains

Hope is what sustained us. The same hope that was ever-present with us while Nathaniel was here is still with us today and available to anyone. Our Divine Daddy's bigger plan was for that hope to take wings and grow in the lives of others. It became Nathaniel's purpose, his legacy, his gift to the world, and it celebrates kids just like him—VIP kids.

Rick Warren says, "In God's Garden of Eden, even broken trees bear fruit." God has a purpose for every life.

With this realization came the birth of Nathaniel's Hope. Nathaniel's purpose would be far greater than anything we could ever imagine.

Nathaniel's Hope celebrates kids with special needs (VIP kids). Kids with varying abilities. Kids with unique abilities. Kids whom God has crafted and created with purpose. We're here to cheer on VIP kids and their families, as well as educate and equip the community and churches to welcome and assist these families as they run their marathon. If you are not a VIP, then you are invited to participate as a Buddy Friend.

Nathaniel's Hope has four core programs:

1. **VIP Birthday Club** — VIP kids around the world are celebrated with a Bearing Hope plush bear upon their enrollment and a card on their birthday! VIP kids who have relocated to their heavenly home are remembered in the Hall of Hope. Their pictures can be posted online, and cards are sent to their parents on their birthdate and home-going date.

2. **Buddy Break** — This Parents' Day Out/Respite program enables VIP kids and their siblings to have fun, while their caregivers get a much-needed break. Nathaniel's Hope is building a national network of churches to provide *free* respite care through Buddy Break. Online training is available.

3. **Make 'm Smile**—This is the biggest party celebrating kids with special needs… our VIPS, of all ages! This annual community festival, hosted in  Orlando, Florida since 2002, is now expanding to new communities.

4. **Christmas with Nathaniel's Hope**—Nathaniel's Toy Shop provides free toys to VIP kids and siblings whose families are in financial need. Caroling for Kids shares hope and encouragement with patients, families, and caregivers at local children's hospitals on Christmas Day. Caroling Caravans deliver joy and toys to home-bound VIP kids.

For more information, visit **www.NathanielsHope.org**.

"He has made everything beautiful
in its time."
—Ecclesiastes 3:11, NIV

It is our desire to see that Hope continue to grow and expand in communities all over this country and even overseas, in other countries.

You see, hope really does live! Hope is not a tangible something that you can hold in your hand, stuff in your pocket, and pull out when you need it most. It's not the Eveready Bunny, always there to lend a hand. Hope doesn't come from Earth; it's not one of the world's commodities.

Hope comes to us from our loving Heavenly Father— our Divine Daddy. The Bible tells us this: "This hope is like a firm and steady anchor for our souls" (Heb. 6:19, CEV). This hope reaches into the middle of whatever "normal" you may be experiencing. It will grip you tightly, help you hang on through any storm or crisis, and will never let go.

It's a hope that will lead you straight into the eternal hope of heaven. It will take you—and your loved ones—right into the arms of your Heavenly Father. Straight into the eternal life that is filled with indescribable beauty and peace. There will be no more pain, no more crying, no more death.

This life you are living now is one you are just passing through. Yes, it's a marathon, but at the end, your *real life* will begin. When your Divine Daddy welcomes you home, "He will wipe all tears from their eyes, and there will be no more death, suffering, crying, or pain. These things of the past are gone forever" (Rev. 21:4).

God is no respecter of persons. What He has done in our lives, He can do for you.

So never forget this one thing: *HOPE LIVES!*

IF YOU'RE A FAN OF THIS BOOK, WILL YOU HELP US SPREAD THE WORD?

There are several ways you can help us get the word out about the message of this book:

- Post a five-star review on Amazon.
- Write about the book on Facebook, Twitter, Instagram—any social media you regularly use!
- If you blog, consider referencing the book or publishing an excerpt from the book with a link back to my website. You have our permission to do this as long as you provide proper credit and backlinks.
- Recommend the book to friends. Word of mouth is the most effective form of advertising.
- Purchase additional copies to give away as gifts.

You can order these books from Amazon, Barnes and Noble or **www.nathanielshope.org.**